I HAD TO CHANGE

Conquering My Past To Embrace My Future

CHARLET LEWIS

Lady Lisa,

Thank you for your support! I thank you and God for the connection. I know God will bless you on your journey through school.

love,

Published by: TL65

ISBN: 978-0-9995796-0-2

Cover Conceptualization: Charlet Lewis

Cover Design: Yosbe Design

Proofreading: Evatopia

Interior Layout: Book Formatting for Authors

Cover Photo: Angelica Epps

Dedication & Acknowledgements

First, all GLORY to my savior and daddy, Jesus Christ! You died for me, yes me. Your love for me is amazing.

I dedicate this book to my mother, Monika Hayden, who unbeknownst to her, birthed a powerful woman of God, an overcomer, and a warrior. She birthed the woman she always wanted to be, but never could attain. Thank you!

I write because she couldn't.
I write because I have something to say.
I write because the enemy hates it.
I write because I'm an ordinary girl who trusts her extraordinary God.
I write so others can live.
I write because I had to change.
I write because YOU have to change.

This is my story of conquering my past to embrace my future through hope, forgiveness, and love. It almost didn't happen; the enemy almost won; but GOD.

Thank you to my husband and best friend, Tony Lewis. I thank you for believing in me when I didn't. I thank you for throwing away your Rule of 3 just for me.

Most of all, I thank you for loving God above all else. Because of your devotion, you are able to be the perfect husband for me and perfect father for our children. I love you.

To my children: Devonne, Joshua, Jordan and Grace — you are the joy and light of my life. I thank God for choosing me to birth the next generation of men and women of God who will change the lives of so many. I declare and decree favor over your lives.

To my sister, Esther, I love you and miss you. To my Light of Life Church family, thank you for loving me, praying for me, and for your continued support to our ministry. To Regina, my spiritual mentor, sister, mother, and friend – I am grateful for your continued guidance and correction when needed. To my mother-in-law, Mary, thank you for loving me as your daughter.

To my editors: Regina, Deacon Libby and Nikeyta — thank you for your wisdom and time. Bishop Joey Johnson, thank you for your continued guidance through my Grief Recovery journey. To my spiritual parents, Dr. R.A. Vernon and Lady Victory Vernon, thank you for standing in the gap. Whenever I feel like an orphan, I remember you. Thank you for pushing me to be a better me, a better wife, mother and first lady.

I love you all,
Charlet

Contents

Forewords

BY R. A. VERNON, D. MIN.

I Had to Change is an introspective investigation into the life of my spiritual daughter, Lady Charlet Lewis. It is a testimony of how she handsomely handled the many troubles she endured to blossom into the woman of God, committed mother, and devoted wife that she is today, all of which I have personally witnessed.

Charlet tells her story with the kind of self-awareness that emerges only when one has embraced the discipline of processing past pain, the vulnerability of one who has marshalled the courage to share their darkest secrets to uplift another, and the brand of raw honesty that bespeaks both brokenness and breakthrough—a rare combination that will resonate deep in the heart of readers.

Charlet overcame abuse, abandonment, adversity, and all manners of grief. She now shares her journey with admirable authenticity, backed by biblical truth.

Her narrative, while woven with tragedy, is told with generous compassion, extended even to the ones who wronged her, which makes *I Had to Change* all the more worthy a read.

Readers will be reminded of the redeeming value of grace—offered and received—and given a readymade framework from which to address hurtful experiences in their own lives.

R. A. Vernon, D. Min.
The Word Church
Founder & Senior Pastor

BY BISHOP F. JOSEPHUS JOHNSON, II

In, *I Had to Change*, Lady Charlet Lewis tells the riveting and challenging story of her life — a life filled with neglect, abuse, abandonment, loss, and disillusionment. The dysfunctionality of her home of origin contributed to self-hatred. She learned to live in quiet desperation, which eventually began to come out sideways in self-destructive behaviors.

Amid the tragedy that was her life, she came into a personal relationship with Jesus, the Christ. This did not automatically cure her of her self-destructive behaviors, but it began a healing process through a personal relationship with a new Father, Jehovah Rapha, the God who heals.

Through a series of Spirit-empowered choices, she began to heal from the pain of her home of origin and develop a new identity through Christ and the power of the Holy Spirit.

In this book, she not only tells her story with exceptional psychological insight and emotional honesty, but she encourages her readers to make a series of choices towards a new life. In The Grief Recovery Method®, we say "Recovery comes from a series of correct choices."

Today, Lady Charlet is not completely healed, if that is ever possible, but she has traveled a great distance on the pathway of healing and deliverance. She is healthily functioning as a wife, mother, pastor's wife, grief counselor, teacher, preacher, and more.

She is a living testimony that you don't have to allow your circumstances to hold you down. Instead, you can rise above them through a new relationship with God the Father, through Jesus our Elder Brother, and the power of the Holy Spirit. You can pursue emotional health and spiritual maturity through a series of correct choices and perseverance.

I believe this book will help you experience emotional health and spiritual maturity.

Bishop F. Josephus Johnson, II
Presiding Bishop of the Beth-El Fellowship of Visionary Churches
Senior Pastor of The House of the Lord
Author of: *The Ravages of Rejection, Grief: A Biblical Pathway to God, and God is Greater than Family Mess.*

Preface

Change!

I had to Change, or else I wouldn't be here to tell my story. Change has become my favorite word, and yet, ironically in times past, it was the word I most despised. Even though my life was nothing but a series of changes, I craved the opposite. I craved familiarity, uniformity, comfort, steadiness, and sameness. I never received it.

I fought change at every angle it would hit me. I didn't need it, didn't want it, and deep down, I didn't feel I deserved it. The pages you are about to read include my life story. Specifically, how I conquered my past filled with depression, loss, grief, low self-esteem, thoughts of suicide, and failure, and learned how to embrace a life of living in total freedom.

I sat on my gift for so many years even when I first heard a small, still voice whisper, "Write it down." At the time, I had just re-dedicated my life to Christ, but I knew nothing about the whispers of "The Holy Spirit." I just believed it was me trying to soothe myself.

But as I grew in my faith and started listening more intently, I kept hearing the whispers, which turned into screams that were too hard to ignore. The screams would come in the form of the company of women He would surround me with. Women who had become authors, speakers, leaders and teachers and yet, were women just like me.

It took many years for me to accept that "I" had a purpose and the call of God on my life. He chose me for a time such as this.

[13] *"I can do all things through Christ who strengthens me" - Philippians 4:13 (NIV)*

This is the first scripture I memorized many years ago. I used to say it over and over in my head, but it never penetrated my heart. Me, do all things? Never. I felt as though I was never good enough to do anything of value. I had learned to skate by, make it look good, fake it till you make it, but I always felt like a failure. Even in my outward triumphs I felt somehow that I didn't measure up. I tried to will myself to feel good about who I was even when I didn't believe in myself. I always gave up by making an excuse for why I couldn't do what I needed and wanted to do.

Since the age of twenty-one, I had been in counseling off and on for depression and dealing with my past. I had enough sense to know that I needed help, perhaps just an outlet, but I didn't have enough sense to apply what I was learning. I just took it in and never realized that I had embraced the very things I wanted to change about my life. My very first counselor told me that I was a "co-dependent" people pleaser, so that is what I embraced; it is who I became.

Why change now? I had to because if I didn't, you may not change. If you are reading this today, and you find yourself in a place where you don't feel loved, good enough, or called for a purpose, then this book and its message are for you. My prayer is that as you read the pages in this book, you will see yourself and understand that no matter where you are, where you came from, how broken, unloved or insignificant you may feel, God loves you! He adores you and is waiting for you to accept His love and change your life.

After every chapter, you will encounter an opportunity to "MAKE A DECISION". In life, no matter what we have endured, no matter how we came to be, no matter our background, at some point we have a decision to make. We have a choice. The same choice God gave us, either to trust Him or reject Him. God in His Sovereignty gave us free will, which gives us the freedom to choose.

How we respond to the ups and downs are up to us. We decide how we will respond. I know what you may be thinking, "I didn't have a choice with what happened to me, I was young, just a child. I was not in control and had no power." Yes, you are right, there are some things that have happened in our lives that we have no control over; however, we do have control now on how we choose to respond after the storm.

Will we use what happened to us as an excuse for not moving forward and become a victim or will we use what happened as an opportunity to move forward as a victor? No matter what you have experienced or been through at the hands of someone else or some circumstance, now is your time to decide to look up and move forward with God.

It's time to make a decision.

ONE

I Had to Recognize that I'm the Problem

"I'm anointed and I have issues."
— Lady Charlet

WHO ME?

How many people do you know who have ever admitted that they were the problem? How many times have you admitted that it was you? If you're being honest, probably not a lot, if at all. It has taken me almost forty years to acknowledge that I'M THE PROBLEM! No, I'm not suggesting that I'm responsible for what happened to me, but I am admitting that I'm the one who failed to deal with the aftermath.

I am the one who rather than look my issues and problems in the face and choose to deal with them, instead swept them under the rug or pretended they never existed in the first place. I am the one who rather than become better, chose to become bitter. Did this happen overnight? Of course not; it happened over a lifetime of enduring heartache, pain, loss and grief. This can happen to all of us when we choose to pretend all is well with the world and move forward as if nothing is wrong.

I, or shall I say we, stand in the way of change, progress, and growth. There were far too many years I blamed everyone else: my father, my mother, my son's father, my circumstances, my upbringing, my heartache, my pain, my disappointments, my failures, and even my God. No matter the circumstance or what happened, it always seemed to be someone else's fault. If it wasn't a person who was responsible for my disillusionment, it was my health, the time, the traffic, the slowly moving line that now made me late to work. I had no sense of accountability. It was always something or someone else. Sound familiar?

I didn't always see the world in this way. Growing up I always took responsibility. But then, the problem was that I took on everyone else's responsibilities. I apologized for everyone around me and everything was my fault. In an effort to be responsible, I took on everyone else's pain and problems. "I'm sorry" was my middle name. If my father came home late and drunk, I would tell my mother it was my fault because he was mad at me because I brought home a B instead of an A. My father would beat my mother because the dinner wasn't ready and on the table when he came home. It was my fault because she had to stop and help me with my chores, so I would not get in trouble. Everything was my fault and I was always sorry.

There's a big difference between something being your fault and realizing that you are the problem. We can be sorry or we can recognize and take ownership for our part of what has occurred. For so many years, I was on the run from my past that I had what many in the Church would call a "Jonah Problem". There is a short book in the Bible about the prophet named Jonah that is only four chapters long, but packed with many practical lessons. Those words helped me glean who I really was. A rebellious girl who neglected instructions from God, who didn't realize that I was the problem until I ended up like Jonah, in my own proverbial belly of a whale.

I'M THE PROBLEM

In the first chapter, Jonah was instructed by God to go to a city called Nineveh to warn the people to change their evil ways or else He (God) would destroy them all. I am sure if you attended at least one children's church class you know the story. The part about this story that I want to share though has nothing to do with Jonah ending up in the belly of the whale, but everything to do with Jonah's disobedience.

Jonah disobeyed God and boarded a ship going the opposite way. Jonah was on the run from his assignment and from God, just like me and many of you who are reading this book. We are running from our past, from our past relationships, from our past hurts and pains, from our responsibilities, from our future, from saying "I'm sorry," and "I forgive you," from ourselves and even from God.

When Jonah boarded that ship going the opposite way of what God had told him, for a moment he thought he was going to be okay. Why? Because he settled in and went to sleep, so comfortable in his decision. It's the same for many of us. Once we proceed on our own path, we settle in as if we never disobeyed God in the first place. However, God always has a way of reminding us He is still there. This truth presented itself in the story of Jonah, and here is where it gets interesting--God caused a great storm.

4 The Lord sent a violent wind over the sea. The storm was so powerful that the ship was in danger of breaking up. -Jonah 1:4 (GW)

Yes, it was God who sent the storm upon the sea. We have to recognize that God will use storms to get our attention, not as punishment, but many times to get us to shift our focus and to give us an opportunity to look to Him. God gave Jonah a direct command to go and share life with a wicked nation of people, yet Jonah who was not in agreement and in fact, even questioned God, decided he knew better.

I look over my life and have come to regret how many times I decided to go my way after God showed me His way. Like Jonah, I questioned Him and decided my way was better.

Now, I believe that it was neither Jonah's intention, nor mine, to deliberately disobey God. Jonah was a prophet, after all, and his entire life was focused on serving God and being his mouthpiece. He loved God, but couldn't understand why God would want to save a wicked nation, and he believed in his heart that God must be wrong.

How many countless times have we done the same? We end up in relationships and that little voice inside tells us that this is not good. We are put in a situation where someone in authority asks us to do something unethical and we know it's not right, but we move forward because we don't want to lose our job or position. We make life altering decisions knowing it is not for the best, but our feelings and emotions have a greater pull than our trust in God.

Similarly, Jonah was on the ship sound asleep when the storm raged outside and everyone else on the ship trembled in fear trying to figure out what to do. They threw cargo over the decks hoping that if the ship were lighter it wouldn't cause them all to be destroyed, but it was to no avail. They prayed to their gods, but nothing stopped the storm, not until they remembered Jonah.

⁷ Then the sailors said to each other, "Let's throw dice to find out who is responsible for bringing this disaster on us." So they threw dice, and the dice indicated that Jonah was responsible. - Jonah 1:7 (GW)

They had found the problem and immediately went to him and asked Jonah what they should do?

⁸ They asked him, "Tell us, why has this disaster happened to us? What do you do for a living? Where do you come from? What country are you from? What nationality are you?" ⁹ Jonah answered them, "I'm a Hebrew. I worship the Lord, the God of heaven. He is the God who made the sea and the land." ¹⁰ Then the men were terrified. They knew that he was running away from the Lord, because he had told them. They asked Jonah, "Why have you done this?" ¹¹ The storm was getting worse. So they asked Jonah, "What should we do with you to calm the sea?" *¹²* **He told them, "Throw me overboard. Then the sea will become calm. I know that I'm responsible for this violent storm."** *-Jonah 1:8-12 (GW) - Emphasis Added*

Do you see it? Jonah asks them *"Throw me overboard. Then the sea will become calm. I know that I'm responsible for this violent storm."* In other words, "I am the problem."

At that very moment, Jonah recognized that the storm had everything to do with him, that he was the reason for what could end up being a massive shipwreck and he took immediate action, telling the sailors to throw him overboard. I had read these passages so many times and heard sermons about Jonah and running from God for so many years, but I always missed verse twelve until my Pastor Dr. R. A. Vernon preached a sermon titled, "I am the Problem."

As he was preaching, the Holy Spirit started to show me instances in my life where I was the problem and just like in Jonah's case, I was sitting in the belly of a whale, except I made excuses why I ended up there.

I'M IN CONTROL

My childhood led me to believe that I somehow had control over people, especially my parents, mainly because I could morph into whatever I needed to be to keep the peace. I was good at it, almost a master at becoming whatever I needed, in order to survive one more night without yelling, cussing, and fussing about nothing.

If like me, and you grew up in a dysfunctional household where you never knew if all hell was going to break loose or if it was going to be a relaxing family movie night, then you will understand how important it was to become a change agent. I guess it was during those years growing up when I learned that I may not be able to change my circumstances, but I could make myself feel better by blaming someone else.

My mother was the master at the blame game. She always had a reason or excuse for why she couldn't do what I believed she really could. She would speak about her upbringing in post war Germany, being the third of four children where she was regarded as the black sheep. She was always getting in trouble, bullied and laughed at simply because she was told that she was a slow learner. She could not keep up with the rest of her class and she was eventually transferred to a trade school instead of going to high school along with the rest of her class. Whenever she told me her story I could hear the pain in her voice, and feel how she wished that someone would have spoken up and said, "No, Monika you are smart; you just need some extra help." But no one did and this became her perfect excuse that always kept her from being who she truly could have become.

She accepted the limits that were placed on her early on and she was never able to overcome the lie the devil placed over her life. She allowed those limitations to define her entire life. Every time she had an opportunity to move forward and step outside of her comfort zone, she would stop.

I became my mother in so many ways because of the words that were spoken over me growing up. She lived and remained at the level she was exposed to, and the same applied to me. The negative words spoken over my life sank deep into my heart and mind, and became part of who I was and what I identified with. Things like:

"You're not really black."
"You think you're white?"
"You're a bastard."
"Your mother is a nigger lover."
"You're just like your mother."
"You're just like your father."
"You are damaged goods."
"You are stupid."
"No one will marry you now."
"You are a whore."
"You're a disappointment."

Sticks and stones may break my bones, but words can never hurt me. That is a lie from the pit of hell. The Word of God tells us:

[21] Death and life are in the power of the tongue, and those who love it will eat its fruit." Proverbs 18:21 (NKJ)

Words hurt and can cause death, the kind of death that we carry around like a ball and chain connected to our legs. Every time we want to move forward, we look down at the reminder of why we can't run. I can heal physically from being beaten by sticks and stones, but not as easily from the pain of words. They can consume us from the outside in, making us believe that we can't recover from them. These words haunt me when I have decisions to make, when I daydream of a better life, or when I plan for my children's future. Each of the words spoken over my life at one time or another, I had to deal with one by one. I had to attack them head on and dispel them of their lies.

"I am black and I'm proud."
"No, I don't think I am white because I embrace all of my heritage."
"I am not a bastard; my parents loved each other."
"My mother loved my father."
"I am me and not my mother."
"I am me and not my father."
"I am not damaged goods; I am the daughter of the King."
"I am smart."
"The perfect man for me chose to marry me."
"I am not a whore."
"I am not a disappointment."

FEAR – FALSE EVIDENCE APPEARING REAL

Have you felt that there is something you should be doing, but there is a force that keeps you from pursuing it? That is called fear. It is the devil's job to kill us early, if not physically, then mentally and emotionally. Should we be surprised? Of course not, it is the enemy's job.

> [10]*The thief comes only to steal and kill and destroy...*
> *-John 10:10 (NIV)*

If he can convince us early in our lives that we have no power and if he can use the people closest to us to speak death over our lives, he can defeat us over and over again, even if we are Bible believing Christians heading to church every Sunday. If he can strike fear in our hearts early on, it will become our defense mechanism. The very things that we think are here to protect us will eventually kill us. We get hurt and we say, "That will never happen again," so we begin to build walls, until our walls are so high no one can penetrate them and then we say, "I'm so alone."

This is a scheme of the enemy to keep you separated and listening to the enemy. When he can get you alone and get your ear, he has you. It's time to break through the wall of fear.

> [7] *For God has not given us a spirit of fear and timidity, but of power, love, and self-discipline. -2 Timothy 1:7 (GW)*

You must understand that fear does not come from our Heavenly Father, it comes from the devil himself. He wants you to be stuck in fear and it is all smoke and mirrors. Sometimes we fear nothing except the unknown, we don't even know why we are afraid of something, we just feel like we should be because it is outside of our comfort zone. The Bible is clear that God has not given us the spirit of fear, but of power, love and self-discipline.

Power, now here is a word I never thought would be one I would use to describe any part of my character. I thought power was a negative word, primarily because it had been perverted by the people around me. My father used his power to diminish his family.

He used his power to exert his anger, fear and pain on us. He used his power to instill fear and false respect. So, for years I wanted nothing to do with power until I started seeing the word being used in the Bible as a positive word, along with boldness and authority.

*⁷For God did not give us a spirit of fear. He gave us a **spirit of power** and of love and of a good mind. -2 Timothy 1:7 (NLV) emphasis added*

God gave us the spirit of Power and I had the power to say NO! The power to say no to the enemy's lies and the power to say no to dysfunction and depression. I finally had the power to stare fear in the face and say, "No, not today devil." I could use the power of my voice through the Holy Spirit to say no, and so can you. Yes, you!

You can make up your mind today that when fear creeps at your door, you need to slam it shut. It does not come from God so you have full authority to cast it out. Every time you have a fearful thought, turn the thought around and speak the opposite. Let me show you.

Your boss asks you to give a presentation to the rest of the staff and you think, "I can't do this; I can't speak in front of people." Immediately say this: "If he asked me, then I am sure I am ready for this, because I can do all things through Christ whom gives me strength."

God has given you a vision and a desire to start your own business. You have written a business plan; you have scouted out opportunities, you have people in your corner encouraging you, but you are afraid to quit your day job because you are afraid that you will not be able to take care of your family financially. The answer is in the Word of God.

¹⁹And this same God who takes care of me will supply all your needs from his glorious riches, which have been given to us in Christ Jesus.
-Philippians 4:19 (NLT)

God will provide for you; the only way we can fight the enemy is to repeat back the Word of God. Satan tried to tempt Jesus after his forty days and nights of fasting in the wilderness and Jesus defeated him by repeating back the Word of God. We can't beg and plead with the devil to leave us alone; we can't hide under a rock *(or under our covers, believe me I've tried);* and, we can't deny that he is at work when our fears set it. The best and most effective weapons we have are the Word of God and our voice.

OWN IT

It's time to take ownership of your situation today. No matter how you got here, this is a new day and a new start. It does not matter what your past is and what you have done. God's grace allows you to start fresh and I pray that today is your day. What do I mean when I say ownership? It is looking at where you are now and coming up with a strategy to heal, grow, and become emotionally healthy. To own what is from your own doing and to cast aside what someone else has spoken over you is not the truth. It is looking in the mirror and having what the old folk used to refer to as, "a come to Jesus moment". It means taking responsibility for your part in the equation. Allow me to give you an idea of what this looks like from my own life.

One of my favorite sayings used to be, "All men are dogs and they all cheat," and based on what I witnessed and experienced in my life, there was some truth in that statement. My biological father cheated on his wife with my mother and I was conceived. My stepfather repeatedly cheated on my mother over the course of their twenty-four-year marriage. My boyfriends, and son's father cheated on me. Yes, so in my world, all men cheated. But do ALL men cheat? No, of course not, but that was all I had ever witnessed, heard of, and even experienced. I wasn't open to realize that there was an entire other brand of man out there because I was comfortable being in places where things were familiar. At least if I continued to deal with the same type of men, I would receive the same type of results. Remember, I craved familiarity. I was comfortable being given more of the same, even if it hurt.

How is it that we end up in the same relationships over and over again, but with a different person? Same drama, same issues, yet a different person and it always seems to be them, as if we have nothing to do with it. Think about your ex, okay now generally we can give 100 reasons why the relationship ended and it usually ends with it being their fault. But how many times do we sit back and say…"I think it's me; I'm the one with the issues; I'm the one with the problem"?

Many times, we take our mommy and daddy issues and project them on the people that we are in a relationship with. Whether it is a romantic relationship or a relationship with our peers or even our superiors. We tend to project our hurts on unsuspecting people at the precise moment they do anything that remotely reminds us of past hurts. I became very good at it, I had a way of driving everyone away when they got too close and when things got shaky, I shifted into overdrive so they would have no choice but to walk away. Then I could be the hero because I didn't leave, instead they left me which made them the bad guy. I can't tell you how many times I played that game. It's called playing the victim, and boy, was I good at it.

ACCOUNTABILITY

I realized that I was my worst enemy and I could not keep myself accountable. I tried the "God keeps me accountable" route, but I always failed miserably. Finally, I understood that I needed to trust someone to hold me accountable, but who? I prayed and asked God to show me who. I opened myself up for the possibility that I could get hurt but I was tired and willing to take the chance. Well God showed up, but not how I expected.

After my husband and I got married, we mutually decided that we should go to Church, not for any other reason than we believed it was what we should do. We were married with one son and one on the way, it's just the adult thing to do, or so we thought. What we didn't know was that God would honor our decision even when our hearts were not there yet. We joined a church and a new life for us began.

It was there that I grew leaps and bounds in my personal faith walk. It set the foundation for me to read God's Word and to follow His teaching. However, I still felt empty because at this point I still didn't understand who I was in Christ. I followed the rules, but I still didn't feel free. It was there that I learned to be rule oriented instead of being grace oriented. It seemed like it was more about appearances. Too many people asked, "How are you?" yet never took the time to look beyond the "I'm fine" response. Even though I felt I was dying on the inside, week after week I served, week after week I followed the rules and traditions, week after week I worked on my outside and neglected my inside. I became the good church girl.

I submitted to my husband because I had to, not because I loved God and did it unto Him. I dressed up, and even wore white stockings and shoes even though I hated them. I didn't talk about my past because I feared being talked about or judged. After some years of serving in ministry, we were asked to go through Deacon Training and I believed that I was only asked because of my husband. I had convinced myself that the church really wanted him and I came with the package.

Surely, I wasn't ready to lead anyone or ready to be in a position of such honor. Me, a Deacon? I didn't read the Bible every day; I didn't know how to pray. I certainly wasn't going to pray out loud. I still held contempt and un-forgiveness in my heart from people that had hurt me. I wasn't qualified, not in the least. I accepted the call reluctantly by telling myself that I'm there to support my husband even though I felt unworthy and unqualified. I was ordained and followed the rules and my duties. I didn't get close to the other women, even the ones I served alongside with mainly because I was scared that if I got too close they may meet the real me and realize that I indeed wasn't qualified. I kept my distance, until I met *her*.

I had just miscarried baby number two a few months after our Jordan was born and I was a mess. The women in church tried to comfort me by telling me things like: "It's God's will," "At least you have other children," and "Count it all joy." Although those may had been spiritually correct statements, none made me feel better. In fact, they made me feel worse. No one spoke to my current emotional state. Not until my husband called the one person I didn't like, did things change.

We had just had another falling out when he handed me the phone and said, "Regina wants to talk to you." I pushed away the phone and said, "I don't want to talk to her." He just stood there holding the phone, and I immediately thought, what will she think of me if I don't get on the phone? I finally got on. I can't remember the conversation, all I remember is how good I felt afterwards. She spoke into my spirit. She didn't even mention the baby. She spoke directly to me and my pain. I reluctantly invited her over the following week, so we could talk more.

Why didn't I like her? Well, Regina was everything I thought I wasn't. She had a radiance about her; she was sure of who she was; she was a hugger; she would hug in such a way that would make the hardest person want to cry and call her Mom; she was gentle and thoughtful with her words; she always looked at the bright side and never had anything negative to say about anyone. She was real, transparent, and genuine. She and her husband had been married for twenty plus years so obviously, they knew what they were doing. She was a servant at heart and she was loved by everyone around. She lit up a room like no other. She was that person who you would want to tell all your junk to and you knew that it would never again leave her lips. To me, someone like her was not real, too good to be true. There had to be a catch.

It was a mid-week evening; my husband was at work when the doorbell rang while I was in the full throw of a heated mother-teenage son argument about his attitude. I stopped mid-sentence when the doorbell rang. I turned to my son and told him we will finish this later to which he responded in a very disrespectful way. I turned away and proceeded to get the door with his disrespect lingering in my head.

I welcomed Regina in and asked her to sit and said, "I'll be back." I went back upstairs to deal with my son or so I thought. I told him he needed to apologize and to my surprise he responded by yelling at the top of his lungs back at me. "Oh, no, you are not going to talk to me like that," I yelled and we argued back and forth for about ten minutes or so. I had enough and started to cry and yelled back at him until I remembered that she was downstairs hearing everything. I didn't know what to do, I was so embarrassed. Here I am a "Deaconess", a woman of God, yelling, using profanity and acting a complete fool. I sat on the steps trying to figure out what to say. I was found out. Now what?

I walked into the kitchen with tears in my eyes and apologized. She looked at me and said, "What for?"

Did I just hear that right?

She looked at me and said, "I want you to be you; stop pretending." As we continued to talk, she ended with telling me that during her prayer time, God told her that she needed to lighten my burden. She said she didn't know what that meant, but she was going to be obedient and whatever it meant she was up for the challenge if I was too. I said yes. She became my accountability partner, and eventually my friend and even my mother *(when needed)*.

WHO ARE YOU ACCOUNTABLE TO?

We are to be accountable to God, but to see what that looks like we must practice it, and how do we do that? By practicing and being accountable to another person. Left on our own, we will always believe we are right! There is a proverb that has helped me every time I think I can do it on my own;

[12]There is more hope for fools than for people who think they are wise. -Proverbs 26:12 (NLT)

That's powerful, there is more hope for fools than for someone like me who thinks that I am wise. As far as I was concerned, I knew it all, but time has proven that I don't, or else I wouldn't have been making the same mistakes again or ended up in the same mess I tried to get out of in the first place.

What I need most in my life is accountability or else I am left up to my own wisdom and if truth be told, if left to my own devices, I will make decisions based on how I feel and not what is true and when I waiver, I will make myself believe that God is in agreement.

You need accountability because if you choose not to and choose to only be held accountable to God, you will eventually follow your heart instead of leading it with God's Word. Left to my own will I will always be the fool. Once I understood Proverbs 26:12, I was able to allow someone in to hold me accountable.

"Success in life, to some great extent, is your willingness to follow instruction." Dr. R. A. Vernon, D. Min

We all need instruction and someone to be accountable to, but we cannot allow just anyone to hold us accountable. When we are accountable to someone else we must be open for correction and even rebuke when necessary. Yes, that is the hard part of being accountable because we don't want to hear "no", or "not yet", "slow down", or "you are wrong". Truth is, we don't know as much as we think we do.

All you must do is look at the Word of God. We fear criticism so much that when the people that hold us accountable use criticism in-love, we are ready to quit and sever the relationship. One thing I have learned is that there is some truth to all criticism, and we must be honest with ourselves and be open to look beyond what we see and even feel.

In the beginning of our accountability arrangement, she would lovingly listen to my drama of the day and then pose me with a choice. Choice A would be to continue my path and Choice B would be a simple question: Are you following Christ? She never gave me the answer or told me what to do, she listened and then asked questions. When I came to her with issues I had with others, even my husband or children, she never took sides. She wasn't the girlfriend who responded with, "Girl, no he/she didn't, if I were you, I would…". No, never! She always guided me back to the Word of God even when it hurt, and yes it hurt most of the time, to the point that I would get mad and avoid her calls. But I was growing and believed what Proverbs 12:1 says:

15

[1] Any who love knowledge want to be told when they are wrong. It is stupid to hate being corrected. -Proverbs 12:1 (GNT)

What a word right there, I was growing and wanted to gain knowledge and here it was in black and white. If I wanted to continue to grow, I had to be corrected when I was wrong or going down the wrong path. The last thing I wanted to be was stupid. I had been called that all too often and had worked too hard on how I felt about myself that I was not going to allow my pride to stop me from being corrected even if it hurt. I had to tell myself when I was in my feelings, that Regina was telling me things out of love and not because I was a bad girl, but because she wanted better for me, she wanted me to live in freedom.

If you want to be held accountable you will have to learn to be corrected and even disciplined. I look at it this way…my heavenly Father loves me so much, that he sent this woman into my life, that wanted nothing from me except to see me grow and be used by God. Since He sent her, then I will honor her position in my life and listen to and apply her correction.

At the end of each day we must be open with ourselves and vulnerable enough to allow someone into our lives to help us grow. Hiding under your blanket, praying to God for Him to do what you want Him to do, will not solve your struggles or issues. Instead, being transparent with yourself and others will. If you believe you are mature, yet run or make excuses or rebuke the person who tries to correct you, I hate to tell you, but YOU, my dear, are not mature.

MAKE A DECISION:

Today, I will be honest with myself and decide that I am the problem that is keeping me from moving forward. Starting today I will take responsibility for my thoughts and my actions. I will no longer blame my circumstances or people in my life; I will take accountability for my choices, my actions, and my responses. I give up full control and give it back to God, for He is the only one who directs my path. When fear tries to creep in the door, I will defeat it by speaking the Word of God over my life. I will ask God to show me who I am to be accountable to and I will work on establishing such a relationship.

_____

Signature

_____

Today's Date

TWO

I Had to Go Back to Go Forward

"We are products of our past, but we don't have to be prisoners of it." — **Rick Warren**

"The past is a place of reference not a place of residence."
- Lady Charlet

My mother used to say, "The past is in the past." It wasn't until I became an adult and began to uncover the things that she had endured that I understood why she lived by this mantra. Her past was ugly and painful and the only way for her to deal with it was to forget about it. Unfortunately, this is something I picked up from her, my thoughts, tendencies and truths from her way of thinking. But I realized early on that I had trouble with that, I didn't like keeping things in, I wanted to shout my pain from the rooftops but I didn't know how and I was scared. What if no one believed me? Or worse yet, what if no one cared?

DEATH AND LIFE

In 2011, my life was coming to a screeching stop. My mother had passed away a few months earlier and three days after her passing we welcomed a beautiful baby girl, our fourth child into our family. I was both devastated and joyous, yet devastation and depression won most days. Most mornings I woke up to my baby girl lying next to me, cradled at my breast, but I couldn't even feel the least bit of joy because somehow if I felt joy it would mean that I wasn't grieving over my mother.

I don't remember much during the first year of her life. I couldn't tell you the first time she smiled, rolled over or even sat up, but what I do remember is pain, sorrow, and most of all, guilt. Guilt that I didn't do enough to help my mother in those last days. Guilt that somehow if I had just fought harder with the insurance company or the doctors I could have made them come up with alternative treatments. Guilt because I wasn't attentive to my husband and my other three children. Guilt because I neglected them, myself, my baby, my church, my job, my health and my GOD. I couldn't read His Word, I couldn't pray, and I didn't dare go to church. I felt guilty because I wasn't the spiritual woman with great faith that I had believed I was and later found out I was pretending to be.

The enemy's lies came fast and hard. I had lost hope in God and in myself, and before I knew it, the enemy was working overtime to bring back all the lies that he had told me my entire life. I didn't deserve a prosperous life, I wasn't a child of God *(or else all this misery couldn't be happening)*, I was a mistake, no one wanted me, I did not have enough faith, my prayers were not being heard because if God was really there, He would have heard them and my mother would still be alive. I will never be enough, no one will ever be proud of me, I was a failure, I was being punished for my past, I wasn't a good mother, I wasn't a good wife, and eventually, my husband would leave me because I was overweight and under functioning. I was what my father had spoken over me the day he found out I was pregnant in my sophomore year in college. He called me "damaged goods" and that no man would ever make me his wife.

HOPE THROUGH GRIEF RECOVERY

I felt lost and abandoned, but then a simple statement from my husband changed everything. While sitting in the living room one evening, he looked over at me and said, "I think this is your time to get certified as a Grief Recovery Specialist." My first reaction was one of anger. How could he be so insensitive? I am at my lowest, grieving the most significant loss of my life and he wanted me to help others grieve? I was just about to get stuck there, when I remembered a promise I made to God that if I could afford the next training I would take the class. I sat there quietly for awhile and God spoke these words into my spirit: "The way to your healing is by helping others heal."

Within the next several minutes I had visited the website and registered for the course. After I registered, I remember feeling this sudden jolt of life flow back into my body. I felt peace, love and joy return at the possibilities of what was about to become. A few days later, some fear crept back in as I found my Grief Recovery book and started to brush up on a few of the chapters. I got stuck on the part about going backward and having to share the past to move forward. It is called a Loss History Graph, an illustration designed to show all the losses I had encountered in my life. As I sat on my bed with my journal, I started to write down the obvious: the deaths and miscarriages. But soon after, I found myself with a list that spanned three pages. As I completed my list, I started to cry uncontrollably at all the losses I had experienced in my life, some I didn't even know were losses. Things such as the loss of never having my biological father in my life, the loss of my sister when she moved back to Germany in 1989, the loss of my innocence, the loss of my career, the loss of my best friend, and the loss of me.

Now that I had recognized the losses, I had a conundrum, the false truth that my mother taught me — "the past is in the past" — versus my new reality — "the past will set me free". Suddenly, all the lies I had believed, but never dealt with were staring me right in my face. As my husband would say, "They came up on my porch and rang the doorbell.: I could no longer ignore them, the rug was being lifted, the closets were being emptied and my heart broke into a thousand pieces. Every wound of hurt and pain I had endured was bursting open, the wounds that I had so perfectly bound with care were being ripped open one by one. I remember thinking, how could I possibly grieve these hurts? How will I survive? Then, I heard His whisper once more: "Your season of grief is over, it's time to face the past".

[3] He heals the brokenhearted and binds up their wounds.- Psalms 147:3 (NKJV)

Psalm 147 was written by King David specially designed to celebrate the rebuilding of Jerusalem, it declared God's providential care towards all creatures, in particularly His people. I am one of His beloved and this promise is for me as much as it is for you. My heart was broken, wounds I had many, but that promise changed my life. He and only He could heal me and bind up my wounds, but He couldn't do it until I chose to allow Him. It became clear to me then, that I was the one who must want to CHANGE and that He would do the rest. It would require work on my part, work that I was ready to start tackling.

I was staring my past in the face, and as I was reading and re-reading the book, I was faced with truthfully completing my very own Loss History Graph. This is how the purpose is described in the The Grief Recovery Handbook®.

"The primary purpose of this exercise is to create a detailed examination of the loss events in your life and to identify the patterns that have resulted from them." There are several other reasons for making a Loss History Graph. One is to bring everything up to the surface where we can look at it. Buried or forgotten, losses can extend the pain and frustration associated with unresolved grief. Another is to practice being totally truthful. We can often be dishonest without ever lying. That is, we omit things and thereby create an inaccurate picture"[1].

"The past cannot be changed, forgotten, edited or erased; it can only be accepted." – author unknown

I tossed and turned many nights thinking about my past, my losses and the griefs that I had experienced. Many nights I cried myself to sleep mourning the little girl inside of me who so desperately wanted to be held and loved by her father. At some point in my life, I had decided that everything I had endured was a direct result of my actions or non-actions. I decided unbeknownst to me that I was in control of other people. How did I end up in this dysfunctional family and how would I change my patterns as not to repeat and pass on the lies I had learned to my children?

GERMANY

I am the second daughter born to my mother in Germany in 1973. I don't have many early memories of spending quality time with my mother. She was there but not the way I wanted her to be. My mother was a party girl. She loved men, alcohol, and occasional fun with drugs. I wonder now was it because deep down inside she felt lonely, scared and invisible? Maybe, just maybe she was looking for love and to be accepted. My sister, Esther, who was four years older than me, was being raised by my grandparents for reasons I still don't understand *(everyone seems to tell a different story)*, so when I came along it was just my mother and I. I knew I had a sister, but there was no sisterly bond between us for the first few years if my life.

I very vividly remember the parties my mother would have in our apartment which usually ended the next morning with a new man of the month. I didn't mind though. I reveled in the attention these men gave me. I wanted a father so badly that anyone who would pay me the slightest attention would do, and without even knowing, I created a pattern that I would take into adulthood. My mother and I lived in a housing project in a small town about a thirty-minute drive from Frankfurt and the nearest Army base.

As a young child, I never really noticed the looks and stares I got from others, all I remember is my mother complaining about it. What I do remember is everyone wanting to touch my hair. As I got older, however, I started to hear the whispers and looks other women would throw at my mother and then the all-out assaults of calling her a "nigger lover".

It was then that I realized I was different; I wasn't like the other blonde, blue-eyed girls in my class. I was one of the few "negger" or "schwarze" kids in our town, translation "nigger" or "blackie". I was the only black child in my family, even my sister was white. We had the same mother, but different fathers. My family thankfully never acknowledged my difference, yet they never even thought to ask me how I felt about it. I don't remember the moment that I realized that I didn't look like everyone else but it started to bother me somewhere around grade school when I started to pay attention to my appearance, my hair and clothes.

I was different and the biggest difference I saw was with my hair more than my skin color, mainly because my mother didn't know how to "tame" *(as she would say)* my hair, so she decided to just cut it. From the time, I was about five years old my hair was kept in a short afro. Was it easy to maintain? Of course, but I didn't look like the other girls with their long, flowing hair. It took many years, about forty years for me to love the way God created my hair - natural thick curls. All the years prior to my final revelation included me straightening, dyeing, perming, adding hair, cutting hair, wearing wigs, snap on ponytails, and braids, you name it, I tried it. But what stuck with me the most was the fact that I looked different than anyone else. Did my friends and family treat me differently? No! But when I looked in the mirror, I saw it. I saw the difference and I didn't like it.

Growing up, I saw many dysfunctional things, things that any young girl should not have seen or been exposed to. I remember my childhood room, the yellow wallpaper, the white furniture and the toys. My bed was positioned right underneath a window and at night the streetlamp from outside always cast a shadow into my room that made me scared. By the time, I was about five-years-old, I remember always sleeping under the covers, shaking in fear until I fell asleep. I'm am sure that is where my fear of the dark started, and fear that I still deal with. My mother would go out and party many nights leaving me at home alone overnight. I have memories of waking up in the middle of the night and walking through our dark apartment searching for her until I realized once again, I was alone. I usually settled in my Mom's bed and cried myself to sleep. It was during those years that I started having dreams — reoccurring, vivid dreams that at times, turned into nightmares. I dream in color, can wake up, go back to sleep and continue my dream. It took me many years to come to the realization that God used and continues to use dreams to speak to me, reveal things, and show me things that He wants me to understand and know.

Because of my mom's lifestyle I never lacked companionship, my mother had lots of friends and even more boyfriends, which I didn't mind. I realized that I was fueled by attention and because I was the "cute little black girl", I always made sure that I was the center of attention. My mother's "man of the month" always seemed to take interest in me and I reveled in the attention they gave me, which created a pattern and mindset that if I'm a "good little girl", people would love me more. I could somehow control them to love me, but love never seemed to last.

My mom, *(as I repeated later in my life)* used her body to receive love and once her man got tired of that, he was gone. What happened in my mother's life that set this pattern? I don't know for sure, but I can speculate. During the last few months of my mother's life she shared many stories of her early childhood, which included her feeling like she didn't matter. She had an older brother and sister who were both respectively smarter than she was. They were praised for their school accomplishments, while she was called dumb by her parents and siblings. At some point, she was transferred to an alternative school where children were sent to learn a trade. Her classes taught her how to cook, bake, sew, and take care of a home. I believe this made my mom an over-achiever. I say that tongue in cheek because she was an excellent cook and could keep a house sparkling clean.

Here she was, the black sheep of the family. Is this what made her rebel? I don't know. By the time my mother was nineteen-years-old, she was pregnant with my older sister. My grandparents, believing she was ill equipped to raise a child, literally took my sister from my mother after she was born and raised her. Did my mother resist? Did she fight to keep her? I don't know. I do know that she loved my sister, however I believe that is where the disconnect began in the relationship between my mother and my sister. My mother wouldn't become the primary caregiver of my sister until years later.

LOVE LOST

In 1972, my mother met and fell in love with a wonderful man. He was a soldier, handsome, and he treated her like gold. Her family and friends liked him and he seemed like he would be the one. Before they knew it, I was born. They planned a life together, marriage, more children and eventually he would take us all to America to live the dream. It didn't turn out that way. By the time, I was a few months old, a woman showed up at my mother's front door with an announcement. Surprise! It was my biological father's wife with their two children, and in that moment my mother's heart was broken into a million pieces. I can't begin to understand how this affected my mother. I can only imagine the pain, disappointment, betrayal and embarrassment she must have felt.

Months later, my father convinced my mother that he loved her and wanted to spend the rest of his life with her. He told her he was going back home to divorce his wife and come back for us. My mother was so overjoyed that she orchestrated and threw him a huge going home party in anticipation for his return to her and us. My mother's youngest sister told me once that my mother waited for months for my father to return. He never did. She told me that about a year or so after he left she tried to look for him, but the Army told her that he was no longer enlisted and there would be no way for them to find him. I can't imagine the hurt my mother must have felt, once again ending up a single mother, now with daughter number two.

I believe that is where she started drowning her sorrows in drugs, alcohol and sex, and yes there was lots of all of them. By the time, I was five-years-old I had tasted every type of alcohol – I used to drink what was left over in the glasses from the previous night's party. I would wake up in the middle of the night and walk into full blown orgies – they didn't even stop just told me to go back to bed. Until this day, I love the smell of weed, I guess the way some people would smell the aroma of fresh baked bread or brownies that reminded them of their mother's kitchen, the smell of weed always brings me back to my childhood. When I think of my two daughters today, I couldn't imagine them exposed to what I had witnessed, and what it could possibly do to their spirits.

THE FATHER I LONGED FOR

Somewhere in between all the partying, my mother came home with him. He was there one morning and he never left. He was young, handsome and so much fun to be around, but most importantly, he treated me like a princess. He played with me, took me on bike rides, and acted silly to my mother's dismay. He was nine years younger than my mother, but seemed so much wiser. He was sure of himself and walked in confidence with a small hint of cockiness. He was my perfect daddy, until he didn't get his way or felt he was getting disrespected. He had a temper that would bring him home many mornings with blood stained clothing from club fights the night before. My mother didn't like it as much as I did. I liked it because my daddy could fight and win, or at least I believed he did.

All seemed well. It had been six or more months and he was still there. Finally, I had a daddy that loved his little girl. From the very beginning he called me daughter and would joke that the only reason he was going to marry my mom was because of me. He was my hero, everything I ever wanted. I finally had a father just like all the kids that lived in our neighborhood. I was normal, I was loved, and I belonged.

BUSTIN' LOOSE

Everything changed that night, every whimsical thought I had about our happy family ended abruptly. My father had a rule – no singing or dancing at the dinner table. This was a slight problem for me because prior to his arrival I could do just about anything I wanted to do, when I wanted to do it. Not many rules were enforced when it was just my mom and I; however, now I had to "behave" because of him. As we were sitting down for dinner, my favorite song came on the radio; it was my daddy's song too. Bustin' Loose by Chuck Brown came blaring through our stereo. I remember my mom's reaction very vividly when she quickly turned to me and gave me a look of "don't dance". There almost seemed to be fear in her eyes.

I ignored her and started to sway back and forth, my father joining in expectantly, which made it so much more fun. My mother who was not in a playful mood walked over and turned down the music. As she returned to her seat, my father stood up and turned the music back up, now louder than before and said, "It's her favorite song." As he sat back down my mother once again stood up and turned off the music. This happened a few more times as if happening in slow motion. At one point, instead of heading to the stereo, my father picked up a hardcover coffee table book and proceeded to strike my mother square in her face as she stood next to the dining room table.

The impact was so hard that her nose shifted and blood started to fly everywhere. He continued to hit her in the face until she could stumble away to lock herself into the bathroom. At some point my father and I made eye contact and the look on his face was something I will never forget. I saw anger, hate, and rage with a hint of sadness and sorrow. I don't know how I recognized sorrow at such a young age, but there was a part of me that felt empathy towards him. As soon as I lost his gaze, he walked out the front door.

I GOT YOU

At the moment when our eyes locked, I was a six-year-old who assumed the role and responsibility of becoming my mother's protector and my father's conscience. I kept thinking that if only I had not wanted to sing my song, none of this would have happened. I thought I had control over my parents and the situation. This was my fault, and if I had only been a good little girl I could have prevented this horrible event in all our lives. Unbeknownst to me I was becoming a little god or what I now refer to as "Holy Spirit Jr". But what I didn't know then is that I was fueled by fear. Jackie Kendall writes in her book, *Surrender Your Junior God Badge*, "The more fearful you are, the more controlling you will be".[2]

Control is an outgrowth of fear, and this was so true for me. I lived in constant fear and therefore, I tried to control everyone and everything around me. I put the weight of the world, my parents, my family and my friends on my shoulders, and that somehow made me believe I could control what happens around me and what others did simply by me being everything to everyone else.

After my father left the house, I helped clean my mother up, consoled her and stayed up the entire night looking out of the window into the parking lot hoping my father would come back. Despite the fact, that he hurt my mother, my father was gone and it was my fault. I promised myself that if he came back I would be such a good little girl and make sure that this would never happen again. He did come back yet despite my best efforts, it kept happening. The viciousness, the anger, and the beatings continued, and after each incident I was there plotting how the next time I would be able to prevent it. What I didn't know then was that this was another pattern that I received from my mother, because my mother would make the same excuses as I did. If only she had cooked what he asked for, if only she didn't question his authority, if only she had cleaned the house the way he liked it, if only. She too believed that her actions could tame the beast that was raging inside of my father.

This abuse continued for years to come. At some point the

beating subsided and he opted for emotional and psychological abuse. However, when times were good, they were good. Despite the pain and dark nights, there were many bright days. I still had many fond memories of my early childhood, family trips and vacations. There were so many great things both my mother and father taught me, especially how to love. I know that may seem oxymoronic based on the cycle of abuse that was happening, but my parents loved each other and they loved me. I know what you are thinking, love wouldn't hurt anyone. Yes, you are right, but people do. My father was flawed and unpredictable, he could be loving one minute and erupt into anger the next.

In 1980, my parents finally got married and due to my grandmother's illness and the death of my grandfather we moved in with my grandmother and my sister. For the first time, my sister and I lived together and even shared a room. Oh, how excited I was, but unfortunately that was short lived. My sister had a major adjustment to deal with. For the first eleven years of her life she lived with our grandparents, then our grandfather passes and then her mother, sister and step-father moved in. She resisted and she resisted vehemently, which made it difficult for me to protect her from our father. She rebelled and got in trouble a lot and seemed to be cast out by both my parents. My father had no love for her and he made that very clear. He called me his daughter and her his step-daughter, he treated her as such except in front of company. In public or around other family we pretended to be one big happy family. I quickly came to realize that I really had no control whatsoever.

COMING TO AMERICA

In 1985 my father, mother, sister, our dog Tiffy and I boarded an airplane to the land of opportunity - America - and my life as I knew it was over. I was eleven-years-old and I was leaving my family, my friends, my school, my country and my language behind. I was scared. I couldn't speak English, barely understood it, and I feared the people and the "ghetto" we would end up in. I laugh about that now because I didn't know what to expect. My perception of

America was only what I saw on the few television shows we were able to watch. Every American show either showed wealth or poverty, there was no in between. I knew we weren't wealthy so I knew for sure we would end up in a rat-infested apartment in the middle of the ghetto. I knew that my life would change forever, and I also knew that I would never return to my home again.

My mother on the other hand was elated, she finally had her dream realized; she exuded the stereotype. In the small town she grew up, several of my mother's friends had "American babies" and the goal was to get married and move to America. Unfortunately for most, this was not in the cards. They remained in our small town raising their American babies alone, and once you had a "black" baby, the German men were no longer interested in you. My mother had hit the jackpot. Her man married her and vowed to provide for both of her children as his own. I don't believe she ever realized the price we would all pay.

We arrived in Washington, D.C. in June of 1985 and moved in with my grandparents into a small three-bedroom row house. My uncle was living with us as well, so in total there were five adults, three kids and one dog living in tight quarters with everyone sharing one bathroom.

MAKE A DECISION:

Today, I decide to look my past in the face and declare, "You will no longer keep me hostage." My past may not have been what I wanted it to be, what I hoped or desired it to be, but I decide today to move forward examining, grieving and healing my past and allowing myself to feel the pain in order not to bring it into my future. The pain of the past has shaped me into the person I am today. I will commit to complete the work required to deal with my past and move forward as the person God has created me to be. I will ask God to show me the right people I can go to for help. I will reach out to someone who is able to hold me accountable to do the work that is required of me to move forward, whether that is a therapist, counselor, grief recovery specialist, or my pastor. Today I will GO BACK TO GO FORWARD!

_____

Signature

_____

Today's Date

THREE

I Had to Go Through

"The purpose exceeds the pain." – *Beth Moore*

WHY ME?

Why me? Why do I have to go through all this pain? Why? Why? Why? This was my mantra to God for so many years. I didn't understand. I went to church week after week listening to sermons about how much God loved me, yet I felt hurt and betrayed by the God who said He loved me so much. I couldn't wrap my head around how God could love me yet see me suffer and in pain. Then I was faced with hearing Christians around me complaining about what they were going through. What? But we are Christians now, why are we still going through pain? We are supposed to live the abundant life; doesn't that mean no more pain?

I was on a quest to discover the answers and the more I looked, the more I prayed, the more I read the Word, the more I realized that I was not exempt from pain. As a matter of fact, life would continue to give me what it had to offer — trials and tribulations —

but I had to decide how to respond to it and how to use it in my life, and to ultimately discover the purpose in my pain.

[28] We know that all things work together for the good of those who love God— those whom he has called according to his plan. -Romans 8:28 (GW)

I first had to realize that if I was going to believe the Word of God that meant I had to believe by faith that all things (the good, the bad and the ugly) work together for the good of those who love God. I love God, so that would mean me. I had to trust Him to use every experience to produce something good within me and to eventually use it to help someone else. These experiences weren't just about me, but also about what they could produce in and through me, if I allowed them to. My first step was to acknowledge my past, realize I had to go through every experience and declare that I would find the purpose in each one of them.

GERMAN GIRL

I had made it to the end of middle school after three very difficult years of trying to cope coming from a German lifestyle and adapting to the American way of living. I left Germany a fifth grader who played with dolls and watched cartoons to entering a seventh-grade D.C. middle school where conversations revolved around sex, drinking and drugs. The cultural shock was great, and because I didn't want to be the "German Girl" as I was called forever, I became a chameleon, becoming whatever I thought I needed to be to fit in or be accepted. I went from being the only black girl in class in Germany to being the only German girl in America. Again, I was different, this time not due to the color of my skin, but for the language I still had trouble understanding and speaking.

German Girl, that is what they called me and I hated it. I didn't want to be different, I wanted to be like everyone else. Of course, everyone was curious about the girl who couldn't speak English fluently and didn't understand the language with its slang and vernacular. Not only did I have to contend with being the German girl but I was also the mixed kid and being in an all-black neighborhood, at times was very uncomfortable. Because my mother was white, I wasn't considered black. I was called "Half Breed", "Oreo", and "White Girl" and told if we were back in slavery times, I would be a house nigger and my father would have been lynched. I never understood why there was so much animosity for children like me. I was a product of two adults making a decision, but now I had to deal with the aftermath. It didn't just happen at school, I saw it also around the streets of D.C. when my family and I would go about our day. My mother always got those "You don't belong here" looks from black women or my father would get the "traitor" looks. Where and how do I fit in? I was too black for Germany and not black enough for America. I lived by what the world was defining me as. I had no sense of self or who God had created me to be.

In my immaturity, I learned who and what to be based on my environment. I leaned on what I knew and that was take control and become whatever "others" wanted me to be. At home I was the obedient child that stayed out of trouble, did my homework, did my chores, and stayed under the radar. However, outside of the house I created and re-created or better yet, morphed into whatever I needed to be to be considered "cool'. I just wanted to be accepted not for being different but for being just me. It never occurred to me that being ME was just enough. I started to hang out with the "cool kids", and did whatever they did.

I missed my home, I missed my grandmother, and of course I missed my friends. The tension of all of us living together under one roof constantly seemed to come to a head, someone was always arguing at some point throughout the day. There were days where it felt like a war zone, never knowing who or what would explode on any given day. After three long years, finally, the day had come and we moved into our first house.

INNOCENCE LOST

My father was very controlling and needed to know where my

mother, my sister and I were at all times. We couldn't leave the house unless he knew where we were going, who we were with, and exactly what time we would be back home. In our house being 60 seconds late would come with dire consequences. He wouldn't take things away or revoke television privileges. Our consequences would involve a belt, an extension cord or sometimes a fist. Even today I generally arrive 10 minutes early for everything because of the repercussion I endured when being late as a child.

One particular weekday my father was working later than usual, so I took the opportunity to go out with a friend of mine after school. Whenever my father was not around, my mother would allow my sister and I more freedom and leniency. My friend invited me to go to a boy's house that she knew I had a crush on. He was an older boy already in high school, and he and his friend invited her to come over. Once we got to his house, it was just the four of us sitting around talking, laughing and having fun. I was nervous, yet excited to be in his presence. For the first time, I felt accepted and normal, even though there was a small part of me that knew I shouldn't have been there. I dismissed my gut feeling and tried to relax. At one point my friend and the other boy got up and went into one of the bedrooms and I was left alone with my crush. I don't remember the conversation but I remember my heart beating, my hands getting clammy and fear starting to rise up inside of me. All I wanted to do was run out of the house, but I didn't want to leave my friend, so I stayed. At one point, he took my hand and led me into the basement where we sat on a raggedy, moldy-smelling couch. I remember how cold and damp the basement felt, not cozy or inviting, but stark and scary. He leaned over and started to kiss me; I froze.

He kept whispering in my ear, "I know why you came over here" and "I know you want this". He unbuttoned my pants and pulled them and my panties down to my ankles and laid me back on the couch. I screamed NO but he didn't hear me, I was only screaming in my head. I was in shock; I didn't know what to do. I wanted him to get off me, I wanted to fight and scream, "No, get off me," yet I just laid there frozen. He got on top of me and preceded to have sex with me while I laid there with tears streaming down my face. It hurt so badly, and I wanted him to stop but I didn't know what to do. While he was on top of me his friend walked in and announced that my friend got scared and left. I was alone. She left me alone; she abandoned me. Why? They both started laughing and my crush asked, "You want next?".

At that moment, I felt like I was a having an out of body experience. I just laid there, scared to move, never saying a word. Once his friend finished, he said to me "German girl, I knew you were cool"! "You need to get up and out of here because my mom's on her way home".

Why didn't I take control? Why didn't I stand up for myself? Why didn't I say no? I thought back to having taken control when my father abused my mother or when I had to protect my sister from my father but now I had to go further; I now had to take control over my body. Never again would I allow anyone to take what I didn't give him.

As I walked up the block to our house, I saw my father's car and immediately grew into a panic. I knew that there was no way I could tell him what happened because this was my fault. I wasn't supposed to be there, I wasn't supposed to go over to a boy's house, especially an older boy, and certainly I wasn't supposed to have sex. It never occurred to me that this could have been considered rape. My understanding of rape then was a stranger attacking a woman by force. He wasn't a stranger and he didn't use force. This was my fault for being somewhere I wasn't supposed to me.

I walked in the house expecting a fight or at least getting yelled at but my father just looked at me as he sat on the steps leading to the second floor. I slowly squeezed by him and met my mother upstairs in their bedroom. Something was wrong, I could feel it. My mother looked at me with tears in her eyes and said, "Pops died". My grandfather had passed away from a massive heart attack earlier that day while cutting the grass. I turned around and went to my room, she turned around and asked me, "Are you okay?" I mumbled something like "Yeah".

I went into the bathroom to clean myself up because I was bleeding heavily. Within a few minutes my mother burst into the bathroom and demanded to know why I was bleeding, so I lied and told her I had just came on my period, to which she responded "Liar". She started yelling about how she knows exactly when my sister and I were starting our cycle and I had already had mine this month. She got in my face and said, "I'm going to ask you one more time, why are you bleeding?"

I wanted to yell back that I didn't want to have sex, I didn't know what to do, I didn't know that I could say no, but nothing came out except: "I had sex." She yelled, "I knew it! You and your "grown ass", she then proceeded to use other expletives that played over and over in my mind for years. I remember thinking how hypocritical she was, wasn't I just following in her footsteps?

My anger towards her grew that day and we grew further apart. I always felt that she chose her husband over us and I was angry and now when she had an opportunity to show me some love and compassion, she once again let me down. As I went to my room to lay down, I started to think about how I wished my conversation with my Mom should have gone. I wished she would had taken me into her arms and said, "It's okay, tell me what happened, I love you and I am here for you". I so desperately wanted her to see me as the girl that had lost her innocence, the girl who would never be the same.

10 For if my father and mother should abandon me, you would welcome and comfort me. -Psalm 27:10 (TLB)

Oh, how I wish I would have known and understood that scripture then. So many nights I felt abandoned by my parents with no comfort in sight. I had to learn to cope on my own. Beloved, if you are feeling abandoned by your father, your mother, your loved ones, your child, your husband, your friends, please know that He, yes, our Heavenly Father, will never abandon you and He will comfort you even when you don't see Him. He has never forgotten about you; the only reason you may feel that way is because no one ever told you He was there.

LIFE LOST

A few weeks shy of my sixteenth birthday, I met my first "boyfriend" and he was no boy. He was eight years older than me and he wanted me. Looking back now, of course he wanted me, I was a gullible young girl who wanted nothing more than to have a "man" tell her "I love you". Our love was real, or so I thought, we would be together three years until the fall semester of my freshman year of college. I never noticed the signs of jealousy – he would always say no one will ever have me again, we will be together until death. He wanted to know where I was every minute of the day and when I didn't answer his page *(yes, this was early 90s and we didn't have cell phones, but pagers)* or phone call, we would argue. I would skip school and spend the entire school day with him at his mother's house. He was everything to me. He was interested in everything I was interested in. He heard me and paid attention to me. He only had eyes for me, he told me he loved me all the time and I gave him all of me whenever he wanted, even when I didn't want to. We planned a future together, marriage, kids, house and a dog. We had it all planned out, yet it never occurred to me that I was planning a future with a drug dealer, someone who couldn't keep a job, had no tangible goals or aspirations to be better. He only talked about a job and never a career, no plans to get out of the drug game, yet I was infatuated with him and couldn't see myself without him. He had a hold on me that I couldn't shake. It took months of ignoring his calls, looking over my shoulder and threating to put a restraining order on him, for him to finally let me go.

In my senior year of high school, I became pregnant and we were so excited. I could get out of my parents' house. It was a perfect solution to finally get out from under my father's abuse and my mother's constant contempt for me. It was a few weeks before my senior prom and my mother confronted me with what I already knew. She looked me square in my face and said, "You're pregnant." I looked down and answered, "Yes."

I expected her wrath, but she just turned and walked away. For days, she gave me the silent treatment until one evening my father looked at me at the dinner table and said, "Your mother told me that you are pregnant. Don't worry, we will take care of it." Wait, what? That was it? I was expecting hell and brimstone to come my way, and the all too often laying of hands. Yes, I was close to being an adult and my father would still physically hit me when he deemed necessary, especially when he was drunk or high.

A week or so went by and on a Saturday morning my mother told me to get up, get dressed and get ready for a doctor's appointment. I was elated, my first prenatal visit! My father, mother and I pulled up to a large gray building with the words "Planned Parenthood" on the marquee. It wasn't our regular doctor I thought, but then our regular doctor was not an obstetrician, so it never occurred to me what was coming next. My father stopped the car, let us out and drove away. My mother and I walked through the doors, checked in and sat down in silence. She didn't say a word; she never even looked my way. After what seemed like a lifetime, someone yelled: Charlet Hayden – NEXT! The nurse called my name and I motioned to my mother to come; she shook her head no and proceeded to flip the pages of a magazine she was reading.

I walked in and was told to undress from the waist down, lay down on the table, open my legs and that I would feel some discomfort but that I needed to lay still. As I laid on that cold sterile table, I felt once again that I was having an out-of-body experience. I saw myself, a scared little girl praying to God to save her. The pain was unbearable and the sound of the machine never left my mind and the tears that started to flow never came to a stop. Sometime after the procedure, I realized the devastating reality – I had an abortion. I walked out of the recovery room with tears in my eyes, got in the car went home and not another word was spoken.

HE SAVED ME

That night, I couldn't sleep because of the abdominal pain I was experiencing and I went into the bathroom. I caught my reflection in the mirror and I hated what I saw. Overcome with grief, I wanted it all to just end. I opened the medicine cabinet and saw my mother's pain pills. Without thought I screwed off the top and emptied the contents into my hand. I didn't make a conscious decision to kill myself, I just wanted the pain to stop and if that included me dying, so be it. Who would care anyway? My parents would probably be too self-absorbed to even care, my sister had a new life in Germany, she would get over it quickly and my boyfriend would find someone else.

I took the pills, and sat on the cold bathroom floor asking God for forgiveness and then asking him a simple question - If you are real, save me. I woke up the next morning in my bed, having no recollection of how I got there. Did God save me? Did my parents save me? As I was laying there lost in thought my father came in my room and yelled, "If you can have sex, you can get up and clean this house." With that I got up, held my emotions in and cleaned the house, all the while knowing without a doubt that it was God who saved me that night.

Not another word was spoken about that day or that night. My parents and I pretended as if it had never happened. My boyfriend who was very upset, decided as well that it would be best to pretend as if it never happened. We made a conscious decision to forget about it. I didn't talk about it and soon it was as if it never happened. It became a faded memory that I buried deep within my heart. The only thing I knew and kept in my heart from that experience was the feeling that it was God who saved my life, as for the rest, the best thing was to bury it and pretend it never happened. There would be no reason why it should ever come up again, right?

NO CONDEMNATION

Wrong! Buried and unresolved grief always has a way of showing up when we least expect it. It could be right away or it could be many years later as it was in my case. My husband and I were still considered newlyweds and here we were with a six-year-old, a one-year old, a new business and a new house and surprise, we were pregnant again. We were nervous yet happy, but it was short lived because within the first trimester I suffered my first of four miscarriages. My doctor reassured me that this wasn't anything out of the ordinary, that it happens to many women, especially ones who had already had children, nothing she said though made me feel better. Nothing! Because all I could think about was that this must be the punishment for the abortion. Even though at that point in my life, I had accepted Jesus Christ as my savior, was going to Church religiously, I was sure that this was the repercussion of my sin.

I prayed and asked God to help me, I asked for forgiveness over and over but I didn't believe that He forgave me, and the more I read the Bible the more the enemy was convincing me that I was right. I kept thinking back to the Old Testament stories of God punishing the sinners including the children and the children's children. I felt stuck and started to question my faith until I came across this passage:

⁸ So now there is no condemnation for those who belong to Christ Jesus. - Romans 8:1 (NLT)

No matter what I've ever done, there is no condemnation in Christ. Christ sits at the Father's right hand, not as an accuser, but as an advocate willing to give His life for me and you. I had to understand that God loved me so much that He gave His son to die for me. If He was willing to do that, would He not also be willing to forgive me for the abortion and my sins? Yes, of course He would and He does. I had to remind myself that condemnation comes from only one source and that is our enemy, the devil, it comes straight from the pit of hell. If the devil can convince you that God has not forgiven you, or that your sin was so great He couldn't possibly forgive you, or you are struggling in the same sin over and over, you will always be stuck in condemnation. When we go to God, acknowledging our sin, asking for forgiveness with a repentant heart, HE WILL FORGIVE us and here is the best part - He remembers our sin no more:

³⁴"....because I will forgive their wickedness and I will no longer hold their sins against them." -Jeremiah 31:34 (GW)

That is the Word of God, if He does not hold our sins against us, then why do we or why do we allow others to remind us and then condemn us with our old sins? Because we are human and we are not like God, but we must continue to remind ourselves that there is no condemnation in Christ.

MAKE A DECISION:

Today, I decide to take the pain I have endured over my lifetime and use it as a stepping stool for motivation and greatness. What the enemy meant for evil, my Father in Heaven will use it for good. The pain and trauma I have endured or even caused will from now on be my testimony that will set someone else free. Lord, please forgive me of my sins _____ *(list the ones you have not asked for forgiveness for)* and repent. I believe that you have forgiven me and I believe that there is no more condemnation in you.

_____

Signature

_____

Today's Date

FOUR

I Had To Stop Lying

"You can't have the true peace of Christ's Kingdom with lies and pretense." - Peter Scazzero

"You can't keep lying to yourself and expect your life to change." - Charlet Lewis

Lying has become so normal in our world today. Everyone does it, we tell ourselves. We give it little pet names like "a white lie", or "a little lie". Turn on television and we see politicians lie, business leaders lie, celebrities lie, and news anchors lie. We lie to get out of work, to be liked, we lie on our taxes, job applications, about how fast we were driving, and we even lie to ourselves - with that said, it should be no surprise that lying is just as pervasive for us Christians. How's that? We lie when someone asks us, "How are you?", we lie and say, "I'm okay". We lie when we hug someone in Church with a big smile, knowing deep down we do not like them. We lie when we say we are too busy to volunteer at Church when the truth is, we just don't feel like it or we have something more exciting happening. We lie when we tell someone they look nice, when we really think the opposite. We lie when we tell everyone our marriage is fine, when in reality our marriage is falling apart. The list goes on and on, and we have gotten so familiar living our lies that we don't even recognize that we are really lying to the world, to God and to ourselves.

PICTURE PERFECT

My dad would always tell me, to get ahead in life, you had to fake it till you make it. He would tell me that if I didn't know the answer, just to make it up, the more you talk the more they will believe you. Lie if you must. Always make yourself look good. He was all about "outside appearances", and he was the master. He would tell us that "what happens in this house, stays in this house". It was made clear that all that mattered was appearances, it didn't matter how you looked or felt on the inside, if you looked like you had it all together on the outside you were just fine. Our family was the "Picture Perfect" family. We were a middle-class family, my mother didn't have to work, my father had a great career and was on an upward track in his profession where he received many noteworthy accolades and recognitions in his field. We were your typical middle class suburban family and he was respected and well-liked by his peers, a generous and all-around family man. He had built a perfect family on the outside. However, things were far from perfect on the inside and behind closed doors. If you had the opportunity to stay longer than a few days with our family you would start to see some things come out sideways, whether it was through a discussion, disagreement or worse yet, an altercation.

As I ripped off the scab of being "Picture Perfect" I realized I had ingrained this pattern as well. I too suffered from the perfection syndrome. I wanted the people I was around, the people I went to church with, worked with and was friends with to believe that I and my family were perfect too. I was married to a wonderful man and our marriage was perfect. We have four beautiful, respectful and successful children, we were generous, our business was successful and prospering, we were financially set with no debt and we were living the good life and we lived to serve God.

Well that's what I wanted people to think, but that was the not the truth; our life wasn't perfect, our marriage had many ups, downs, bumps and bruises, our children were far from respectful at times, our business was barely afloat, and we were drowning in debt. Somehow, I had myself convinced that my idea of "Picture Perfect" was acceptable because unlike my father I was not an alcoholic, a drug addict, a narcissist, or an abuser. I was everything God was creating me to be and yet still it wasn't good enough for me. I still didn't feel God's love for me.

WHO ARE YOU?

Over the next few weeks, after starting my grief recovery work, memories of my past started to come back into view, and with painstaking effort I recorded each memory in my journal. Early one morning I woke up to a voice in my spirit that asked: "Who are you?" All day I pondered the question. I didn't have an answer, I wanted to scream, "I am the righteousness of Christ", "I am a daughter of the King", "I am loved, I am worthy" yet nothing came out. It's what I wanted to say, but not what I felt. Me righteous? Me a daughter? Me loved and worthy? At this point in my life I had created exactly who I wanted to be.

I was a loving wife, a mother who cooked dinner every night, kept the house tidy and neat, went to work, organized and paid the bills, was my husband's cheerleader in whatever endeavor he was working on and most importantly, was a woman of God that served His people even to exhaustion. I realized then that I was just like my parents, pretending for the world yet falling apart on the inside, hating the very thing that we tell people bring us joy. I hated what I had become: a pretender, a people pleaser, an over-functioner, a liar and a fake. I felt as though there was nothing authentic about me. Days turned into weeks and I still pondered the question, "Who are you"? As weeks turned into months I decided to write down in my journal every time I felt positive about myself or something I did that made me feel good about myself. Before I knew it, my list started to grow. I would sit at night and read and re-read the words I had written and decided that even though I didn't feel some of them any longer, that they were still true.

WHAT HAPPENED TO YOU?

My husband looked at me and said, "What happened to you?" It was as if he was staring into my soul, as if he could see me naked and exposed. All my mess, all my tragedies, all my trauma right there spilled all over the kitchen floor. What happened to me? Life happened, abandonment happened, betrayal happened, hurt and pain happened, loss happened, low self-esteem happened, abuse happened, and yet I was unable to tell him any of it. I just stared at the floor and said, "I don't know."

This was one of many fights we had early in our marriage. We had only been married for less than a year and truth be told, I think we both wanted out. Neither one of us was happy, our idea of marriage was not what we expected or had hoped for. What happened? Life? Now there's an easy answer, because it's the easiest to grasp. Ask yourself, how many times have you answered someone when they asked you why you are not living your dream? Why your marriage is where it is? Or why you haven't pursued your dream? Life happened…gotta make a dollar out of fifteen cents. Story of our lives.

Our courtship was magical, a true love-at-first-sight type of story. Anyone who has been around us long enough has heard the story of how we met, and how we both called our mothers and told them, "I just met the person I am going to marry." My husband tells the story so much better to the point where our daughters ask for him to tell the story over and over. We met at the gym, exchanged phone numbers and the following Saturday we went out on a date and from there on, we were inseparable. Only problem was that he was engaged and living with his fiancée in their townhome that they jointly owned. Now for most, that would be a red flag and a very good reason to move on, but I had hope that he would be the one.

THE "OTHER" WOMAN

Despite the red flag, I made it clear to him that I was not interested in being in another relationship where I was the "other woman" or "side piece". Prior to meeting my husband, I had just gotten out of a long-term relationship with a married man. Yes, a married man, I don't write this boastfully instead with much trepidation. I had convinced myself that being the other woman was the best position to be. I called the shots, I got what I wanted when I wanted it, I was always the object of his desires and so on. Basically, I believed all the lies the enemy convinces us of when we are living in a way that is contrary to God's Word. Now I could make the excuse that at the time I was in this relationship, I wasn't living for Christ even though I was saved, or that this is what I saw my father do, so I was only emulating the behavior I saw. But there was no excuse. I knew it was wrong. It was wrong when it began and it was wrong when I ended it; however, I convinced myself that I wasn't hurting anyone.

Truth is, I wasn't looking for the relationship, it wasn't my intent to be with a married man, but we worked together, spent time together, had similar interests, and he complimented me often. He was like my "work husband" who I would tell all my single dating horror stories to, which he would respond with, "If I was your man…" and in turn he would tell me about all the things his wife was not doing, to which of course my response was, "If I was your wife…"

It didn't take long for the friendship to turn into a sexual relationship. Every time we parted ways I was depressed. I wanted the life he was going home to. The spouse, the kids, the house, the dog, the family vacations, the dream. So instead, I convinced myself that I was more important because he was willing to risk his marriage to be with me. Crazy, right? The mind is amazing, you can justify anything if you really want to and I was ready to justify this affair. The devil is called many things including the father of lies, and here I was in the middle of a big lie. Affairs, adultery exist in a realm of lies. He lies to her, he lies to you, he lies to himself, you lie to the world, you lie to yourself and then you cry to yourself because there will be nobody left to lie to. I was lying to myself and I finally decided I had enough.

I prayed and asked God to help me get out of the relationship and He honored my prayer. Thank you, Jesus. A few months after I ended the relationship, I met my husband. I had made my mind up that the next man I would date, I would marry. I was tired of the single dating life, I was tired of getting it wrong, so I decided to stop dating and decided to trust God.

FINALLY, THE "ONE"

I knew the moment I met him, that he would be the one, but he was attached so I gave him an ultimatum. Her or me? Shortly there-after, he ended his relationship and within three months we moved in together and six months later we got married, and six months later we had our first son together. Fast? Oh yes. Would I do it all over again? Absolutely! Did we have problems early on because we rushed it? Heck yes! We both walked in blindly hoping and praying for the best without discussing or planning what we were doing; we just did it. We just believed that everything would work out. We were in love and that is all you need, right?

TROUBLE IN PARADISE

Wrong! We realized early on that in order to make a marriage work, it takes so much more than just love. But what I didn't know was what it would take, so I decided to step back into my old ways of "Picture Perfect". I started pretending that all was well, especially with family and friends, since it was them who thought that we were moving too fast. I wanted to prove that we knew what we were doing. I went into full pretense mode. We were the perfect family with a house, two cars, two kids, and a business. We were going to church and living the dream.

But beneath the surface brewed all our unresolved issues. My father, mother, abandonment, loneliness and depression issues and his "I'm the head and you better submit" alpha male, only child syndrome and abandonment issues. We were a blended family and we had no idea how to properly blend on top of financial issues of starting a new business, my job lay-off, and a new house.

We had only been married less than a year and we were at a point where he didn't want to come home and I didn't want him to come. It all came to a head on September 11, 2001, when he screamed at me during a heated argument and said: "I am not your father," and continued with, "What happened to you"? I was discovered. I immediately knew I had to stop lying and pretending that everything was okay. It wasn't.

We started talking about divorce. I told him I wasn't ready for this because I was so damaged, that I needed help, counseling, therapy, I didn't know what, I just knew I needed something. I was living a lie. We sat and talked all morning until we could no longer ignore the repeated phone calls from my parents, which we didn't want to answer because they were a huge source of our issues. I finally answered the phone to my mother crying and asking me to turn on the TV. We got off the phone, turned on the TV and for the rest of the day watched in shock and horror, the unfolding of that tragic day we now memorialize as 9/11.

As we sat and watched, we both realized that the issues we were dealing with were minor in comparison to what was happening in the world. "What if one of us would have been lost that day," we asked each other? We decided that day, that the word divorce or the "D" word as we refer to it now would never be mentioned again. There was no plan B which meant we had to resolve our differences, get the help we needed as a couple as well as individually. However long it took, we would commit to be the best version of us we could be. We decided to stop lying to each other, voice how we felt and heal.

When we decide to lie - to others, to ourselves, whether it is to impress others, make ourselves look better or smarter, we are walking into a trap that the enemy uses to get us to live in condemnation, fear and bondage. When I want to impress people more than I want Jesus, it will always show a serious heart problem within me. Essentially because what I am saying to God is, that I do not trust Him to help, heal, or deliver me of my issue. I choose rather to align myself to the father of lies *(satan)* rather than be honest and ask God for help.

COUNTER THE LIES

How do we counter the lies that we have believed about ourselves? How do we counter the lies that others have spoken over us? If I was going to stop lying to myself, I had to identify the lies that the enemy was throwing at me and then learn to fight the lies with God's Word. The enemy is relentless with his lies and we must be equally relentless to cling to the truths of God's Word. We must be vigilant in discerning how satan tries to deceive us. If you are dealing with any of the following issues below, you must know that these are the work of the enemy in your life and that you must identify, confront, and counter with God's truth:

Fear	Offense	Guilt
False Guilt	False Accusations	Condemnation
Doubt	Misinformation	Anger
Temptation	Deception	Lies
Discouragement	Disappointments	Depression
Hostility	Worry	Anxiety
Division	Conflict	Hurt

Jesus modeled this perfectly for us when He showed us how to counter the enemy's lies when in the wilderness with a bold "it is written" rebuke, we see this exchange in Matthew Chapter 4:3-11.

[3] The tempter came to him and said, "If you are the Son of God, tell these stones to become loaves of bread." [4] Jesus answered, "Scripture says, 'A person cannot live on bread alone but on every word that God speaks.'" [5] Then the devil took him into the holy city and had him stand on the highest part of the temple. [6] He said to Jesus, "If you are the Son of God, jump! Scripture says, 'He will put his angels in charge of you. They will carry you in their hands so that you never hit

your foot against a rock.'" ⁷ Jesus said to him, "Again, Scripture says, 'Never tempt the Lord your God.'"[a] ⁸ Once more the devil took him to a very high mountain and showed him all the kingdoms in the world and their glory. ⁹ The devil said to him, "I will give you all this if you will bow down and worship me." ¹⁰ Jesus said to him, "Go away, Satan! Scripture says, 'Worship the Lord your God and serve only him.'" ¹¹ Then the devil left him, and angels came to take care of him. -Matthew 4:3-11 (GW)

This is the blueprint on how we are to deal with the lies when faced with them. We counter the lies with God's Word. We cannot, let me repeat, we cannot fight the enemy on our own, neither with our will nor our intellect. We can't ask him nicely to go away, we can't beg and plead, we can't will, wish or hope the enemy away. The only way we can fight the enemy is to use the Word of God. How does this work in my life? Your life? Let me show you.

When the enemy tries to convince you that:
You are nothing!
You are useless!
You're not good enough!
You'll never measure up!
Your past is too ugly or dirty!

You must counter these lies with truth from God's Word. When the lies creep in your mind, stop and reap the following:

I am alive with Christ. -Eph 2:5
I am a new creature in Christ. -2 Cor 5:17
I am the righteousness of God in Christ Jesus. -2 Cor 5:21
Greater is He who is in me than he who is in the world. -1 Jn 4:4
It is not I who live, but Christ lives in me. -Gal 2:20
I am greatly loved by God. -Rom 1:7; Eph 2:4; Col 3:12
I can do all things through Christ Jesus. -Phil 4:13
I am more than a conqueror. -Rom 8:37
I am God's workmanship. -Eph 2:10

MAKE A DECISION:

Today, I decide to stop lying to others and myself. I will acknowledge who I am – the good, the bad and the ugly, and focus on the good and expose the bad and the ugly. I will stop rehearsing the lies that the enemy has spoken over my life and I will start to speak the Word of God over my life. I will not strive for perfection but strive for a healthy me. I will stop pretending and faking it, instead I will be honest with God, others and myself. Today, I decide to stop lying and instead, live in total freedom.

_____

Signature

_____

Today's Date

FIVE

I Had To Change My Mind

"Your mind is a powerful thing. When you fill it with positive thoughts, your life will start to change." Author Unknown

[2] Don't copy the behavior and customs of this world, but let God transform you into a new person by changing the way you think. Then you will learn to know God's will for you, which is good and pleasing and perfect. -Romans 12:2 (NLT)

It hit me like a ton of bricks...I was copying my parents' behaviors instead of allowing God to change the way I think. It never occurred to me that Christ could change the way I think. Yes, of course, He could change my life, deliver me from sin, keep me from harm and shower me with blessings, but change my mind? I continued to study the Bible and everything the Bible had to say about renewing my mind. Slowly but surely some of the old thoughts started to fall off. Every time I had a negative thought, I made it a habit to replace it with a positive thought. It wasn't easy and I failed many times, but I kept at it. I decided to set a new pattern for myself, a pattern that would come from the only one who could love me unconditionally, Jesus Christ.

THE MIND OF CHRIST

...But we understand these things, for we have the mind of Christ. -1 Corinthians 2:16 (NLT)

I have the mind of Christ? If that was so, how come my mind was always so confused? How come my mind was fixed on my past? My mind seemed to be fixed on the people who hurt me. My mind was cluttered, confused and exhausted.

My mind is where I lived, and since early childhood all I had was my mind. It was my escape when I was sad, angry, upset, hurt or depressed; I used my mind to go to another world. I can remember as far back as my elementary years that I would create a world in my mind. A world where I was loved, had parents who loved and cared for each other, or a world where I was safe and could speak my mind without having to face the wrath of my father's anger or the feeling of loneliness by my mother's non-involvement. I envisioned a world with no yelling, cursing or fighting, but I realized as I got older that the safe place I would create in my mind became the same place I would get stuck in.

Every time I encountered a hurt, betrayal or pain, I would use it as another brick to build a wall, and by the time I was in my mid-twenties, the wall I had built was almost impenetrable.

In my mind is where I shared how I felt and what I thought, never to be heard by the world around me. It never occurred to me that the safe place I created in my mind as a child would later keep me bound as an adult. Every time I wanted to speak up for myself, assert myself, it was my mind that told me no. No, I wasn't good enough; no, no one would listen anyway; no, no one really cared about me; no, you can't do that because "what if you fail?".

For months, this scripture resounded in my mind: "I have the mind of Christ". Was this true? If I truly had the mind of Christ, that meant I could change my mind and think like Christ? The Word of God tells us that as a believer in Jesus, we are given the mind of Christ. That is, we can think spiritual thoughts because Christ is alive in us. We should no longer think the way we used to. Instead, we can begin to think as Christ does.

That was a liberating thought, but how would I begin? I decided that every time I had a negative thought I needed to replace it with something positive. Sounded simple enough, but the truth is, it wasn't easy and there are still days when I must be focused and intentional about what I allow myself to think.

SEX EQUALS LOVE?

From as early as I can remember my mind was stuck on finding love and truthfully, I didn't care where it came from or from whom. All I wanted was to be accepted for who I was and to be truly loved. However, my dysfunctional upbringing and experiences didn't teach me what love really looked like, so in my mind I equated sex with love.

I returned the attention of any man who even remotely showed me some affection with sex because I thought that was the way for me to reciprocate the feeling. I couldn't understand why I never had the type of relationships I saw on TV or in movies, because that is what I longed for. I had created in my mind what it would and should look like, but never came to realize that I was building fantasies based on lies. As I got older, I came to recognize that in all the encounters I had, I was being used so my mind told me that for me to "not" get hurt I should assert myself and use them first.

INDEPENDENT WOMAN

I bought into the lie that I was an independent woman who now will "use" before being "used". My motto was "If you gonna call me a hoe, I might as well be a good one." I called the shots, I made the first move, I would love them and leave them, the same way they had loved and left me. The world made this easy for me because almost every TV channel showed young independent women using their sexuality to their advantage. I truly felt in control. Oh, how naïve. How many nights I felt like I had the upper hand or felt in control because I could tell "him" that "he" couldn't stay the night and "he" had to leave my bed and my apartment before the night was over. Don't even think about spending the night because my son was in his room down the hall, and I wasn't going to be like my mother. I thought I was calling the shots, yet each night I cried myself to sleep because I was still alone.

Alone…what a concept! My mind equated being alone with being unwanted. I should have used this time alone as an opportunity to learn to love myself. Even though my mother was unhappy for most of her life, at least she was married and had a man, and even though I was alone at least every now and then I had a man in my bed. I wish I could tell you when I met my husband that my mind had been renewed and I was thinking like Christ. But that didn't happen until years later.

YOU ARE WHAT YOU THINK

Many negative things had been spoken over my life that I started to believe. Even though I kept telling others and myself that I was a healthy young woman, the opposite was true. We can only pretend for so long until someone sees right through us.

During my sophomore year at Howard University, I fell in love once again and became pregnant. My parents wanted me to have another abortion, but this time I used my voice in opposition. My parents gave me an ultimatum – have an abortion and we will continue to pay for school or have the baby and you will have to drop out. The answer was easy. I dropped out and had my first child, Devonne, a son.

A few years after my parents finally got over my decision, my father, thanks to his business connections, helped me get my first "real job" at a tech company. I was hired to answer phones and to run errands. After a year, the company grew and so did my position. I still answered the phones but was relied upon by many of the other employees to get things done administratively. I was a hard worker, loved to serve others and wanted to move up, but I was still a little rough around the edges in the way that I dressed and chose to conduct myself at times.

Until one day someone took notice. When you work hard and your motives are pure, people will take notice. They may not say something right away but eventually they will pay attention. That is exactly what happened to me when God allowed a co-worker to notice my work ethic and she would eventually help me see myself in a different light.

Her name was Karrén; she was a young black female boss. She was refined, intelligent, bold, beautiful, savvy, well dressed, independent and awesome at her job, but what I really looked up to was her sense of self. She knew who she was. Even though she and I were the only two women in the entire company, she never backed down and didn't use her femininity as a tool to move ahead. I looked up to her and she spoke into my life like no one ever had. She never sat me down and said "Okay, I'm going to mentor you or tell you how to move up the corporate ladder." No, she just started encouraging me, giving me pointers and suggestions on how to be taken seriously. She never told me I was not dressing for success; instead, she invited me to go shopping with her. I asked questions and she answered. I did well and she applauded; I messed up and she corrected me. She didn't overlook my mess-ups.

Every time I told her I couldn't do something, she told me I could. Every time I would tell her of my past, she would say "So what!". She would give me a positive for every negative. She would build me up when I was down and she believed in me. She saw the potential in me that I didn't. She taught me how to stand firm even in moments of criticism. Within another year, I moved from the admin position to a technical recruiting position, thanks to her motivation.

My relationship with her allowed me to see a parallel in my relationship with God. He saw me as righteous and perfect in Him. We see the mess, but He sees beyond. We see our past and our present; He sees the finished project. God used Karrén to impact me even at a time when I didn't know who He was.

WHAT'S YOUR PATTERN?

To change my mind, I had to kill the negative patterns I had ingrained in my life. Those past thought patterns that were all so familiar. What is a pattern? According to the dictionary a pattern is anything fashioned or designed to serve as a model or guide for something to be made and a form or model proposed for imitation.[3]

Since a pattern is anything designed to serve as a model for imitation, what happens when you model or imitate something that is wrong? It is like when we say, "Practice makes perfect". Does it really? What if you practice spelling a word that is misspelled? All you have done is practiced spelling it wrong. It doesn't matter how long or how often you practice if what you are practicing is incorrect.

Our reasons for doing what we do are often based on what and how we have been taught. It's our pattern. Our parents, our guardians or our extended family that raised us instill their patterns in us as our first teachers. They set the patterns for our lives and as we grow, we either decide to allow them to become our truth or we decide that they are lies and we oppose them. I had so many patterns that were stifling my growth and keeping me in bondage.

Bringing all my faulty and dysfunctional patterns to the surface was not something I wanted to do, yet I made a decision to remove the Band-Aid. It was time for me to deal with the dysfunction. I thought leaving it in the past worked but I realized that my buried and forgotten issues would surface when I least expected them to. They surfaced when I was faced with struggles, when I was going "through" and in the late midnight hours staring at the ceiling when I couldn't sleep.

These patterns caused me pain and frustration, yet it didn't seem as bad because no one knew about them. I was never honest with the people I loved, because if I truly told them how I felt or what was going through my mind, they would surely think I was crazy. I became good at lying to myself and others painting myself as a powerful, smart, strong woman of God. I had set a pattern of masquerading that could only lead me to a path of isolation and destruction. What patterns have been ingrained in you? What patterns are you following and why?

My pattern of engaging in destructive behavior fueled my inability to handle conflict. I modeled what my parents did. Instead of talking, they screamed; instead of being respectful, they were demeaning, and verbally and physically abusive. I shied away from any conflict or resolution. Instead, I created a new pattern of "conflict avoidance". I just ignored it *(Don't try this at home)*. It didn't work and only exacerbated the problems further. What started as a molehill was now a mountain because I was afraid to deal with conflict. I had seen and been a part of so many verbal and physical fights that after I left my parents' house I made a declaration that I was done with that. I would be civil, understanding and mild mannered. But this translated into becoming the ultimate people pleaser and conflict avoider. But it seemed at every turn, whether at home, at work, at my children's school or even at church there was conflict.

I kept praying and asking God to remove these conflicts from my life but nothing changed, to which I realized that the reason nothing was changing was because God was using these conflicts to teach me how to change destructive patterns. One morning during my devotional time I read Matthew 18:15-17.

[15] *"If a believer does something wrong, [a]go, confront him when the two of you are alone. If he listens to you, you have won back that believer.* [16] *But if he does not listen, take one or two others with you so that every accusation may be verified by two or three witnesses.* [17] *If he ignores these witnesses, tell it to the community of believers. If he also ignores the community, deal with him as you would a heathen or a tax collector. -Matthew 18:15-17 (NLT)*

I continued to study the subject and came across an article on the Focus on the Family website written by Mary J. Yerkes. She shares the following three steps when confronted by conflict, based on Matthew Chapter 18:

1) Speak up. If your brother sins against you, go and show him his fault, just between the two of you *(Mat 18:15 NIV)*. God calls us to be peacemakers, not peacekeepers, she points out peace might mean risking conflict to bring about a genuine peace *(Ps. 34:14; Heb. 12:14)*. Speaking up is very different from venting, which can have negative consequences. We should speak the truth to someone in love after we have spent time praying and preparing for our time together. Approach that person in gentleness and with humility *(Gal. 6:1)*.

2) Stand up. But if he will not listen, take one or two others along, so that every matter may be established by the testimony of two or three witnesses *(Matt. 18:16)*. God calls us to stand against sin, evil, deception, abuse and wickedness. When others are blind to their sin, God calls us to enlist the help of others. With a supportive person or church by your side, say, "I will not continue to live in fear", "be lied to", or "be degraded."

3) Step back. If he refuses to listen even to the church, treat him as you would a pagan or a tax collector *(Matt. 18:17)*, says Jesus. In biblical culture, Jews did not have close, personal relationships with pagans and tax collectors. Vernick says when someone refuses to respond to our concerns, the relationship changes. "You cannot have fellowship with someone who refuses to respect your feelings, doesn't care about you, won't respect you and who isn't honest." When we step back from the relationship, it helps minimize the damage and gives the other person time to reflect on his behavior and the relationship. It sends a message that a pattern of sinful, destructive behaviors is unacceptable to us and to God.[4]

GARBAGE IN GARBAGE OUT

When we think garbage in garbage out we usually think about our bodies and healthy eating. There are certain foods that help stimulate our brains and makes our bodies healthy and then there is junk food which when eaten daily will create junk and chaos in our lives because with it comes: weight gain, health issues such as high blood pressure, obesity, diabetes, heart attacks, you get the picture. The same is true in what you see, what you hear, and what you allow into your mind. I think Proverbs 15:14 reflects this sentiment beautifully.

> [14]*A wise person is hungry for knowledge, while the fool feeds on trash. -Proverbs 15:14 (NLT)*

If I was going to renew my mind I had to be hungry for knowledge and pay attention to what I was filling my mind with, and what I was thinking on a continuous basis. I had to literally identify what I was thinking about and go one step further. I had to start guarding my mind and thoughts and stop feeding on trash. What was my thought life like? Was I thinking negative or positive thoughts throughout the day? When conflict arose or things didn't go as planned, did I think positively or yet again negatively? I had to realize that I had a choice! Years of being around negativity made it easy, even natural, to be focused on the negative. It was my default response. I wanted to renew my mind, so I did what I needed to do to break the destructive patterns in my mind.

I continued to read God's Word and found help meditating on Philippians 4:6-8.

> [6] *Never worry about anything. But in every situation let God know what you need in prayers and requests while giving thanks.* [7] *Then God's peace, which goes beyond anything we can imagine, will guard your thoughts and emotions through Christ Jesus. -Philippians 4:6-7 (GW)*

I was being told not to worry about anything. ANYTHING! But in every situation to pray and let God know what I needed and then to thank Him. Why? Because I needed to believe by faith what I just prayed for would be done according to His will, and then I would have peace. I understood the scripture but I wrestle with how long it would take for me to receive the peace He promised. It wasn't until I decided to stop trying to figure out God and decided to trust Him, that I started to guard my mind and be conscious of what I was allowing myself to think.

⁸ Finally, brothers and sisters, keep your thoughts on whatever is right or deserves praise: things that are true, honorable, fair, pure, acceptable, or commendable. - Philippians 4:8 (GW)

The scripture goes on to say what I should think about, things that are "true, honorable, fair, pure, acceptable, or commendable". It was that simple, and I realized that I had to retrain my mind, and refrain from negative thoughts, complaints, worries, and lies. I had to filter everything through these words. Is what I am thinking about right now a truth or a lie? Is it honorable or dishonorable? Is it fair or unjust? Is it pure or polluted? Is it acceptable or unacceptable? Is it commendable or reprehensible? If it was garbage I had to throw it out, right then and there. The scripture told me to pray about everything and I have noticed that the more I pray, the less I worry. This was a reminder to me to pray continuously throughout the day.

This required practice, commitment and consistency. Was this an easy thing to do? No, but I knew I had to continue if I was going to break the pattern of negativity.

As my walk with Christ became stronger, I realized if I wanted to learn more about Him, and if I wanted to understand the Bible for myself instead of just chewing on the few passages that I listened to at Church, I had to read it for myself. Quite frankly the Bible intimidated me. The only version I was aware of was the King James Version and as many times as I picked it up to read it, I always put it back down because I didn't understand it. I tried to read it cover to cover, but I had never made it beyond Leviticus.

It wasn't until we started going to our first Church that I was introduced to other versions of the Bible. Who knew? I purchased an NIV and NLT version and I started to fall in love with the Word of God. The Bible finally started to make sense and God started to illuminate my mind and spirit. I realized the more I read the Bible the more I learned and the more I could deal with the issues of life.

RENEW YOUR MIND

²Don't become so well-adjusted to your culture that you fit into it without even thinking. Instead, fix your attention on God. You'll be changed from the inside out. Readily recognize what he wants from you, and quickly respond to it. Unlike the culture around you, always dragging you down to its level of immaturity, God brings the best out of you, develops well-formed maturity in you. -Romans 12:2 (MSG)

You must ask yourself, the same way I had to ask myself, do I fit in with the rest of the world without thinking? Am I doing the same things as non-believers? Is my attention focused on things of this world more than on God? Am I more thoughtful of planning my week based on what shows come on television, what time the game comes on or what night is happy hour or girl's night out? Is the world dragging me down to its level? Am I still making the same immature decisions I made before I accepted Christ? Or do I want to be changed and renewed from the inside out?

As much as I want to watch certain television shows, go out to the movies, and hang out with my friends, the question always remains in my mind, will those activities allow me to grow in Christ and renew my mind? I am not suggesting not having down time, or enjoying time with your family and friends. What I am suggesting is to pay attention to how you spend your time and how you are investing in learning and growing. The Bible tells us to fill our minds with the right things. How? By reading the Word of God and spending time with Him.

Not sure how to get started on renewing your mind? Here are a few suggestions:

1. **Quiet your Mind** - Be intentional about creating time alone. Get into a quiet space *(hide in the bathroom, especially if you are a mother)*. This isn't a time to be busy; it's a time to slow down. Psalm 62:5 (NKJV) says, "My soul, wait

silently for God alone, for my expectation is from Him."
In this passage, David tells his soul to be silent or quiet
before God, and we need to do the same.

2. **Focus your mind on Him** - This will require some
   work. If you are not purposeful to focus your mind on
   Him, then you are allowing your mind to go where it
   wants to. What helped me focus my mind was Romans
   8:5 (GNT) "Those who live as their human nature tells
   them to, have their minds controlled by what human
   nature wants. Those who live as the Spirit tells them to,
   have their minds controlled by what the Spirit wants."

3. **Pray what's on your mind**. Philippians 4:6 (NKJV)
   says, "Be anxious for nothing, but in everything by
   prayer and supplication, with thanksgiving, let your
   requests be made known to God". In other words, it
   should be as easy to talk to God, as to anyone else. It is
   simply a conversation. Pray about whatever is on your
   mind or is causing you to worry. Just pray about
   whatever God has put on your heart and mind.

The benefits of renewing our mind, by spending time reading
and meditating on scripture, will gradually mature us to recognize
His voice in our lives. It's where He dwells inside of us and we then
can make decisions based on what He is leading us to do, instead of
what we think, feel or want. When I went beyond what I wanted,
what I thought and what I felt, I could renew my mind and come to
a place where the blessings of God were – In His righteousness, His
love, His peace and His joy, they all started to overflow in my life.

MAKE A DECISION:

Today, I commit to renewing my mind. I will identify and break
the dysfunctional and negative patterns in my life. I will no longer
copy the behavior and patterns of this world. Instead, I will renew
my mind in and through Him (Jesus Christ) by reading the Bible,
His Word, and meditating on it day and night, praying instead of

worrying. I will put God first in my life and put my confidence and all of my trust in Him at all times.

_____

    Signature

_____

    Today's Date

SIX

I Had To Change My Heart

"Sometimes God does not change your situation because He is trying to change your heart."
- author unknown

There is a promise that God spoke through the prophet Ezekiel in Chapter 36 , it says:

26 I will give you a new heart and put a new spirit within you; I will take the heart of stone out of your flesh and give you a heart of flesh. -Ezekiel 36:26 (NKJV)

HEART OF STONE

I had a heart of stone because of all the years of hurt, pain, and losses I endured, and I had successfully built walls around my heart so high that it was almost impossible for anyone to penetrate, and even when they did; my heart was just as solid as the wall. The walls and my hard heart gave me a false sense of security that even if someone let me down again, it wouldn't hurt. What I didn't realize was that having a hard heart left me feeling lonely and isolated most of the time, because I was no longer approachable, kind and loving. The way I hid that was by being quiet and telling people I was an introvert. Truth was, I just didn't want to interact because I didn't want to get hurt. I learned to be alone and when I interacted with others, I was always guarded, ready to hurt them before they would hurt me. I would leave the relationship before anything bad could happen. If I had the upper hand I was going to take control of the relationship no matter who it was with, and whenever I started feeling as if my walls were coming down I quickly left and built the walls back up. I had become a master builder; I had become impenetrable.

I LOVE YOU!

"I love you." Why was it so hard for my mother to say these three little words to me? Was it part of the German culture? Thinking back to my life in Germany I can't ever remember my grandmother or any other family member saying that to one another or even to us children. It was as if those three words were only spoken by lovers in movies. It could be possible that no one ever spoke those words to my mother.

The first time my mother said "I love you" to me was as an adult. Growing up my mother was not the mushy, loving, hugging, doting on her kids kind of mom and it left me begging for attention from my father, who was the complete opposite. When he was in a good mood, he was very loving. He would never have a problem saying, "I love you", but often his actions didn't follow his words. He would be loving on Monday and on Tuesday verbally berate me or worse, physically attack me. After many years, his loving words meant nothing. I was growing up in a household where I craved attention from both my mother and father and all the while my heart was getting heavier.

With every hurt, every betrayal, every promise that wasn't

fulfilled my heart became harder. As I look back now at every relationship I had been involved in since I left my parents' house, I can see my desperate need to be seen. I couldn't handle being vulnerable, open and honest because when I tried to be that at home, it was never received or it was used against me. I was in protective mode until I met my husband.

From the moment I met him, I felt as if he could be the one who would rescue me from a life of being alone. He was everything I thought I wanted in a man and yet he was everything that made me feel uncomfortable because he was the opposite of me. He was a visionary, he knew what he wanted, he didn't think about how to do it...he just did it. He was self-confident and had this belief that no matter what, in the end everything was going to work out. His passion, and his keen sense of self drew me to him. I was nothing like that then. I was never sure of myself, always needed validation and never thought that I could make anything happen.

I'M NOT YOUR FATHER

I knew I had to change my heart. I had to let people in. I had to take a chance, but how? It started with allowing someone to love me, all of me. It was our first real fight as a married couple and I didn't relent, I wanted to win the fight. I watched my parents fight my entire life and I knew I was not going to take it sitting down the way my mother did, so I fought and fought hard. Every time he wanted to agree with me to end the argument, I started it again. I called him names, I yelled, I cried, I fought with the intention to hurt him. It was during another argument that my husband stepped back and yelled back at me, "I'm not your father."

I stopped in my tracks as I realized that I was not fighting my husband, but my father. For the first time, I felt I had the power to defend myself, but I didn't realize that I was aiming at the wrong target. I was shocked, embarrassed and confused. What had I become? What was wrong with me? Why was I willing to fight the person who vowed to love me for the rest of my life? Why was I repeating the pattern of my mother?

I immediately went right into defense mode, I rejected what my husband said, and fought back with an arsenal of excuses of why I was responding the way I was. That night I couldn't sleep and kept rehashing his words: "I'm not your Father."

GUARD YOUR HEART

I finally cried out to God and He told me that I had a heart condition; my heart was hard. What could He mean by that? The only time I had ever heard about a hard heart was in reference to Pharaoh when he would not allow the children of Israel to leave for the promised land. What? Was God comparing me to the evil Pharaoh? I was confused and became angry. I was a good person, I went to church, sowing seeds, serving and now you compare me to someone evil. My pity party didn't last long, because I decided to flip open my daily devotional for the day that I had neglected to read that morning, which was based on Proverbs 4:32,

> [23] *Above all else, guard your heart, for everything you do flows from it. -Proverbs 4:23 (NIV)*

The premise of the devotional was that the quality of my life was a direct reflection of my heart. Everything flows from our heart — our hopes, our dreams, our fears, our anxieties, our disappointments, our anger, our forgiveness, our un-forgiveness, our humility, our peace, our greed, our generosity, and most importantly, our love. Yes, everything that makes us who we are is in our heart, and whether we want it to or not it will pour out for others to witness. The writer implores us, above all else, guard your heart. But before I could guard it I had to understand that I could not change it, that was God's job. We cannot change the condition of our heart. Only God can, and He promises to do so if you will ask Him. Remember the words the prophet Ezekiel spoke in Ezekiel 36:26? "I will give you a new heart and put a new spirit within you; and I will remove the heart of stone from your flesh and give you a heart of flesh. Our job is to ask, trust, and receive our new heart.

MAKE A DECISION:

Today, I decide to allow God to change my heart. I trust Him to do the easy work, while I do the hard work of loving, forgiving, and trusting. I will tear down the walls I have built over a lifetime of hurt and pain, knowing that I may get hurt again but believing that God will be there every step of the way. I will love with an open heart instead of a closed one.

_____

Signature

_____

Today's Date

SEVEN

I Had To Grieve

"The Key to recovery from grief is action not time."
- The Grief Recovery Institute

I tried to drink it away
I tried to put one in the air
I tried to dance it away
I tried to change it with my hair

I ran my credit card bill up
Thought a new dress would make it better
I tried to work it away
But that just made me even sadder

I tried to keep myself busy
I ran around in circles
Think I made myself dizzy
I slept it away, I sexed it away
I read it away

I tried to run it away
Thought then my head be feeling clearer
I traveled 70 states
Thought moving around make me feel better

I tried to let go my lover
Thought if I was alone then maybe I could recover
To write it away or cry it away

Solange Knowles - Cranes in the Sky Lyrics[5]

I remember getting in my car one afternoon and my radio station was turned to one of the local hip-hop stations and this song came on. I was just about to change the station, when I heard the first lyric and I couldn't even move my car from park to drive. I was engrossed in the lyrics. I immediately grabbed my iPhone and downloaded the song and for the remainder of the day I listened to the song over and over. She spoke my language; she could put in a song how I had felt my entire life up until I met Jesus. Even though I didn't know what she may have been in need of, my heart went out to her and I started to pray for her.

My entire young life was balled up in those lyrics, I tried everything, love, sex, shopping, drinking, partying, reading, cleaning, moving, you name it, I tried it. In Grief Recovery, we affectionately call this "STERBS" which stand for short term energy relieving behaviors. A STERB is any action, activity, or behavior in which we participate, that creates the "illusion" that we're dealing with the emotions caused by the events and interactions that affect our lives."[6]

Months after my mother passed away, I started my Grief Recovery journey and realized I was becoming good at helping others heal and recover from their grief, even though I was still dealing with the effects of unresolved relationships from my past. I had recovered from my mother's death and the losses of our babies but there were still hidden griefs that I was not ready to face and I knew if I didn't, I would remain stuck. I would continue to relive the pain and hurt that I had experienced. Why wasn't I willing or ready to go back? Yes, you guessed it, FEAR.

Fear raised its head once again and despite everything that I now believed, seemed to have me bound. I prayed and asked God for deliverance and He was ready and waiting to deliver me, but I had to take the first step.

BREAKTHROUGH & DELIVERY

Many times, we ask God for breakthrough and delivery and we pray and hope God to just instantaneously and miraculously take it all away. Of course, He can, but God is waiting for us to do our part. We must believe by faith and we must want it, and we have to activate it. It's like praying for God to give you a job, but you are just sitting at home waiting for the phone to ring, yet you have not put in one application or let anyone know you are seeking a job. Probably not going to happen that way, God expects us to do our part. We can't pray for an "A" when we didn't even study. The Bible tells us that faith without works is dead. If you believe by faith then you have to put in the work. We have a responsibility in our deliverance.

I believe that our breakthrough begins where our excuses end. We say we want to lose weight, but then come the excuses: I can't afford a gym membership, I need someone to do it with me, I don't like to eat healthy, I can't this and I can't that, and so on. We say we want to become financially free, but every sale we see we need to make a purchase because it's "on sale" and we think we are saving. The excuses are ongoing.

We say we want to grow deeper in Christ and have healthy relationships, yet we tell ourselves we don't need to go to church, read our bibles, read books that address our issues, submit to authority (our Pastors, husbands, parents, employers, etc). We say we want accountability until accountability tells us we are heading in the wrong direction.

STOP THE EXCUSES

I believe life begins where our excuses end. What were my excuses? I was afraid of what I would uncover about myself. I didn't want to let go of the comfort of old hurts and pain. Whenever I encountered obstacles, I could use the excuse of the pain of my past. The all-too-familiar "I can't do this, because you don't understand what I've been through" or "I just can't deal with this now, I have too much going on". It was my safety blanket. What about you? What are you excuses for not accepting your breakthrough and delivery?

In the Gospel of John the fifth chapter, we are told about a man at the Pool of Bethesda waiting to be healed. The Pool of Bethesda was known as a place of healing, usually crowded with destitute people who were blind, lame, and paralyzed. One day among them was a man who had been lame for thirty-eight years. Imagine having to deal with the same issue or struggle for thirty-eight years.

6 When Jesus saw him lying there and learned that he had been in this condition for a long time, he asked him, "Do you want to get well?" -John 5:6 (NIV)

On the surface, the answer would seem obvious. Of course, the man wanted to be well or else he wouldn't have been at the pool for the last thirty-eight years, but Jesus was asking a deeper question. He was probing the man's heart. Did he really want to be made whole? Did he really want to be transformed from the inside and out? What happened next is what happens to many of us. We become so comfortable in our situation and even though we want to get out and be healed and made whole, we respond like the man at the pool. He responded to Jesus' question with excuses:

7 "Sir," the invalid replied, "I have no one to help me into the pool when the water is stirred. While I am trying to get in, someone else goes down ahead of me." John 5:7 (NIV)

The man gave two excuses why he couldn't be healed, now they both seemed like valid reasons but he was talking to Jesus. This is the precise moment where his faith should have overridden his excuses. Are you ready to allow your faith to override your excuses? God is interested not in our perfection, but our participation. Are you ready to participate in your breakthrough and deliverance? The only thing that is blocking you is your willingness to believe it is possible. Do what you can, and trust God to do what you can't.

DO THE WORK

I was ready to do my Grief Recovery work, but before I began I asked my counselor to be my accountability person, because I knew if left to my own devices, I would quit at the first quiver of pain. I started to work on one of my first Grief Recovery assignments: a Loss History Graph. "This graph is designed to help you discover what losses have occurred in your life and which of them are most restricting your day-to-day living."[7]

As I was carefully plotting every loss I had experienced on my graph, I quickly realized that I was staring at three pages' worth of losses. Losses that I hadn't thought of in many years and losses I would rather have forgotten. It felt as if I had opened the floodgates of grief. I had completed another step in my healing process but there was so much more to come.

If you've endured a past that you want to desperately forget, I encourage you to dig deep within yourself and push past the fear. Truth is, if you are unwilling to go back, you can't move forward. The past will find you and when it does, it may not be pleasant.

For weeks, I would pick up the pages of losses and just stare at them. Some days I would rejoice, thanking God for allowing me to still be here, but then there were days when I looked at the pages and wept inconsolably at the pain and heartache I had endured. How could one woman endure so much pain and yet still manage to get out of bed every day? I wanted so desperately to live in the freedom Jesus had promised me and I knew that the only way to achieve that was through telling the truth and healing my wounds.

There were so many losses that I wanted to forget, especially the loss of Daniel and the loss of my parents.

After twenty-six years of marriage, my father walked out on my mother for the very last time. His drug habit had finally taken total control over him. He had lost his career, wiped out his savings, and was starting to pawn his personal belongings. Despite the strained relationship I had with my mother, I decided to fly to Alabama where my parents were living, and bring my mother back to live with us. When I arrived at their home, not many things of value were left. My mother packed her clothes, wiped out her bank account, and we headed back to Virginia.

DAD

My mother would always tell me the reason she couldn't leave my father was because if she left, he would die. She believed that she was his lifeline, and only she could keep him from self-destruction. She became his savior. She took control over his life in the same way I had done for her. My mother had lived with us for a little over a year when she was finally ready to go back to Alabama and start a new life on her own. I really didn't want her to go, but I knew she had to, if she was going to learn to live on her own.

About a year later our phone rang early in the morning. It was my mother hysterically crying and yelling, "He's dead."

"Who's dead?" I asked.

"Kenny, I mean your dad. Your dad is dead!"

My heart sank, but a sense of calm came over me. It's over, it's finally over, or so I thought. Even after his death there was turmoil. It took us over three weeks to finally lay him to rest because we had to wait for the army to release his dental records for us to identify his body. My father had died from a drug overdose. His body was found in an abandoned building during a short heat wave in October and by the time he was found, his body had started to decompose and could not be identified. We had to wait.

DANIEL

"I'm sorry, Mrs. Lewis but there is no heartbeat."

This couldn't be happening again. I couldn't lose another baby; we had already given him a name. I was twenty-three weeks pregnant with Daniel and this was the fourth time I had heard the words "no heartbeat". We were ushered into another room to sit with the doctor who tried to explain something that was incomprehensible. I was scheduled for a D&C the next Monday morning, meaning I would have to carry Daniel inside of me for the entire weekend.

Just two weeks prior we received the results of a test that indicated that Daniel may have Trisomy 18 (a condition also known as Edwards Syndrome that causes severe development delays due to an extra chromosome 18). Once I got over the initial shock, I prayed and told God that it didn't matter what disability my son may have, I was up for the challenge and I would love him no matter what. Just don't let him die.

We were scheduled for an amniocentesis to confirm the doctor's suspicion. The day before the amniocentesis we had our regular weekly sonogram at which time Daniel was thriving, moving and kicking constantly. Yet less than twenty-four hours later, we were told that our son had died.

I was numb and angry, why was this happening again? I'd done everything I was supposed to including twice daily heparin injections. It was a year prior that I was diagnosed with pregnancy induced thrombophilia, a condition that clots the blood during pregnancy. This disorder is what caused the prior miscarriages *(blood clots would form in the umbilical cord making it impossible for the baby to receive oxygen)*. That night I laid down and asked God for a miracle. I knew Daniel had died, but I needed to hold him even though I knew that would be impossible. I cried myself to sleep. I woke up with severe contractions around four o'clock in the morning.

I wasn't supposed to go into labor. The doctor said it would be very unlikely, but not impossible. As we checked into Labor and Delivery, I could feel the sadness set in. The doctors and nurses were very professional and understanding, yet they seemed sad. The mood was somber. I was told that I would have to deliver him vaginally and that I would have a chance to hold him if I wanted to.

God had heard my prayer. At 10:24 a.m. that November morning, Daniel was born into heaven. He was small. The nurse wrapped him in a blanket and both my husband and I held him, prayed over him and said our goodbyes. The peace I felt that morning was indescribable. All the pain, anger and sadness disappeared while we held our son.

MOM

I was about six months pregnant with Grace and I was having a meltdown in the middle of the kitchen. It was the end of the summer break and between my husband, the three kids at home, a full-time job, serving in a leadership position at church, and a baby on the way, I was worn out. All I wanted was my mother and she wasn't coming to visit us again until November when the baby was due to arrive.

I called her on the phone crying and asking if she would come early, could she get on a plane this upcoming weekend. To my surprise, she immediately said yes. The very next Saturday I waited at the airport to pick her up. All was well, my life just got so much easier with her being there, until early one morning during breakfast she complained of severe pain in her back and side. The pain came and went for a couple of days, until in the middle of the night she woke me up from my sleep doubled over in pain. I got dressed and my husband and I took her to the Emergency Room. Several days later she was sent home diagnosed with a possible stroke.

She was barely home two days when the pain started again and we took her back to the Emergency Room. Six months prior she had been given a clean bill of health from her oncologist as she had been diagnosed with Non-Hodgkin's lymphoma several years earlier. She had completed her chemotherapy treatments and the cancer was gone. But her pain didn't go away and they ran every test they could to figure out what was going on.

We requested her medical records from Alabama because I had a feeling the cancer was back, but the doctors believed that there was another cause for her pain. Test after test ruled out all the things it might be, so finally a bone marrow test was ordered. The result - Lymphoma and it was in her bones and lymph nodes. Her diagnosis was a 30% survival rate. I was numb, this couldn't be happening. I lost my father a few years earlier, then Daniel, and now here I was eight months pregnant and was being told my mother had only a small chance of surviving.

My mother was finally happy. She had accepted Christ and was loving who she was becoming. I didn't understand. How can this happen? How could God allow this to happen? I prayed and prayed begging God to spare my mother. This wasn't fair. How could He do this to me?

I walked into the hospital room with a lump in my throat and a huge smile on my face.

"Hi, Mom! Grace and I are here," I said as I rubbed my belly. "How are you feeling today?"

"I'm feeling okay. What did the doctors say?"

I responded with "Oh, Mom, same as every day. It's the cancer but we are going to beat it."

"Of course we are. I'm going to see my granddaughter soon," she replied.

We played that game for another month until finally the doctors pulled me aside to tell me what I already knew. The chemotherapy wasn't working. We could send mom to hospice or we could take her home. I decided to take her home, knowing I could never live with myself is she died without me being there.

"Guess what, Mom? They are letting you come home. They think you will get better at home."

She looked at me, smiled and said, "Okay, whatever you think is best."

We both knew why she was coming home, but neither one of us said anything. She came home on a Thursday evening talking and feeling full of life. By the following Wednesday she became quiet and withdrawn, and on Friday, which was my birthday, she was unable to talk. She just lay there staring at me as I opened the card and present she had prepared the week before. The hospice nurse came in daily to check her vitals, medicine and overall state. During what ended up being his last visit, he said, "Get ready."

My mother's longtime friend Patricia came to visit and decided to stay the night to give me a helping hand and to hopefully allow me to get some sleep. She told me not to worry that she would be up with her all night if she needed to be. Around two in the morning she woke me up because she thought my mom was in some discomfort and she wanted me to administer her medicine. I walked in the room and instantly knew that when I walked back out, it would be without her. I sat next to her, holding her hand, and whispering in her ear that it was okay for her to go. We would be okay, she didn't have to hold on for us anymore. I called my sister in Germany and told her to tell Mom whatever she needed to say. I told her I would hold the phone to her ear, but that she couldn't respond. As I held the phone, my mother's eyes teared up as she stared at me. I kissed her forehead, told her thank you for being a great mother and told her I would always love her.

As I sat holding her hand, I felt a sense of calm come over me and silence fell into the room. Her labored breathing had ceased. She was gone. But God was there. I felt Him in my grief; He was there.

¹⁸ *The LORD is close to the brokenhearted and saves those who are crushed in spirit. -Psalm 34:18 (NIV)*

If we believe the promises in the Bible when all is well then, we must believe them when all is not. I knew God was with me that day. He was with me when I found out my father died. He was with me when I was told "there is no heartbeat" and He was with me when my mother took her last breath. But even though He was there, it didn't mean that I wasn't in pain. Of course I was, I was hurt, I was sad, I was angry, and I didn't understand but I believed that He was with me because I was the "brokenhearted", and I believed with all my heart that ALL things work for good, even death.

Unfortunately, our society does not teach us how to deal with grief and loss. It's uncomfortable to talk about it, so we spiritualize or intellectualize it away. We learn to stuff our feelings and put on the brave "I'm fine" face. But Jesus taught the exact opposite. In Matthew 5:4 Jesus himself tell us:

> [4] *"Blessed are those who mourn, for they will be comforted. - Matthew 5:4 (NLT)*

He is telling us it's okay to mourn and to grieve. We're not grieving for their sake, instead we're grieving for our own sake because we're going to miss them. What do you do with your feelings? You must deal with them, you must acknowledge them, you must feel them and you must do the work to release them and grieve the loss. You can't pretend it never happened, you can't stuff them down and away, you can't rehearse them and go over and over in your mind.

No! You release them — you give them to God. You cry out to God, "God, I'm hurt!', "I'm confused", "I'm angry", "I'm grieving"! Grief when left unchecked will fester and seep into all areas of our lives and keep us stuck. I was tired of being stuck and making excuses - I had to do the work. Now it's your turn and your time to release your grief so that God can begin to heal your heart.

MAKE A DECISION:

Today, I decide to grieve all losses in my life, and today I decide to deal with all my unresolved relationships. I will fight against every erroneous thing I was taught about grief and look to Christ to help me make the release. I will search out accountability, a grief recovery group, or counseling. I will no longer run from the pain, instead I will run towards it and do the work required to become a healthy me.

_____

Signature

_____

Today's Date

EIGHT

I Had To Forgive

"Forgiveness is the final form of Love."
– Reinhold Niebuhr

"Forgiveness does not erase the bitter past. A healed memory is not a deleted memory. Instead forgiving what we cannot forget creates a new way to remember. We change the memory of our past into a hope for our future."
- Lewis B. Smedes

How can I forgive if I can't forget? How can I forgive my mother for not protecting us? How can I forgive my father for being an addict? How can I forgive my friend for leaving me alone with them? How can I forgive them for violating my body and my innocence? How do I forgive God for allowing all of this to happen to me?

15 But if you refuse to forgive others, your Father will not forgive your sins. - Matthew 6:15 (NLT)

I must have read that scripture a million times. I wrote it on a sticky and placed it on my mirror as a constant reminder, yet still I despised it. I argued with God over it and I didn't want to apply it to my life. I was mad at God and I refused to forgive, but I knew I needed to. But how? What was the formula? I knew what He expected of me — to say the words, "I forgive you." And I did, yet in my heart I didn't feel it and every time a memory would come up, I was back in the same place of unforgiveness.

I would tell people all the time that I had forgiven the people in my life who hurt me, but it was a lie. Deep down, I still held onto all the pain and misery that I experienced. I couldn't stop asking the same questions in my mind over and over.

How could I possibly forgive my biological father for leaving not only me, but also my mother? I had convinced myself that he was the reason why my mother married my father, he was the reason why my father abused us. It was all his fault. He could have loved us, he could have stayed and protected us, but he didn't. He chose to love his first family more than us. I needed to forgive.

How could I forgive my mother for staying in a marriage for decades knowing that her husband was abusing her daughters? How could she stay knowing that he was continuously engaging in adulterous affairs? How could I forgive her for choosing him over us? How could I forgive her for marrying a monster? I needed to forgive.

How could I forgive my father for emotionally killing my mother? How could I forgive him for abusing my sister? How could I forgive him for forcing me to have an abortion? How could I forgive him for the physical, mental, and emotional abuse he inflicted on me? How could I forgive him for choosing drugs and alcohol over us? I needed to forgive.

How could I forgive my sister for leaving me alone with our parents? How could I forgive her for abandoning me to suffer alone? How could I forgive her for moving back to Germany and escaping what I couldn't? I needed to forgive.

How could I forgive myself for the years of living in disobedi-

ence and living a lifestyle that was so out of order and beneath me?
I needed to forgive myself.

FORGIVE TO BE FORGIVEN

I wish I could say that after reading Matthew 6:15 I had no
problem forgiving, but that would be a lie. I read it over and over,
asking God to help me forgive. I spent hours on the floor wailing
and crying out to Him and begging Him to take the pain away. But
that never happened, not until I realized that forgiveness did not
mean that there would be no pain.

I thought that forgiveness was a feeling. If you are like I was,
then maybe that is the reason you still battle with forgiveness.
Forgiveness is not about the other person; forgiveness is for yourself.

My number one goal for forgiveness was that I could look at
them and say, "I forgive you," and in turn, they would look at me
lovingly and say, "I am so sorry I ever hurt you, please forgive
me too".

Yes, that is what I was waiting for. It wasn't until I went through
Grief Recovery that I realized this is not forgiveness, but instead
manipulation. I wanted so desperately to hear an apology that I was
willing to live with unforgiveness until I got it. The Grief Recovery
Method© taught me that my thought pattern about forgiveness was
pretty normal yet utterly wrong, because it teaches that "an unso-
licited forgiveness will almost always be perceived as an attack;
therefore, it is almost always inadvisable. It will usually provoke a
new issue that will create even more incompleteness. The person
being forgiven never needs to know that it has happened."[8]

I came to realize that forgiveness is not about hearing, "I'm
sorry," but about forgiving that person even if they never knew that
I forgave them. Refusing to forgive doesn't hurt the person who hurt
you, it only hurts you.

FORGIVE OR CONDONE

The reason I refused to forgive was because I thought that I was letting the person who hurt me off the hook, as if what they did was okay, and by forgiving them I was condoning their behavior. I believed that forgive and condone meant the same thing. I literally had to look up the words forgive and condone in the dictionary.

The word forgive means to cease to feel resentment against [an offender], and the word condone means to pardon or overlook voluntarily; esp.: to treat as if trivial, harmless, or of no importance. Do you see the difference?

Cole James with the Grief Recovery Institute says it best: "If we believe the two words to be synonymous, it would be virtually impossible to forgive. The implication that we might trivialize a horrible event is clearly unacceptable. However, if we used the above definition for forgive we would be on the right track."[9] Forgiving is not condoning what they did, instead it is a leap of faith we take to experience freedom that comes as a result of letting go.

As I began to practice forgiveness, I came across a story in the Bible that helped me recognize that I was on the right path. In Genesis Chapters 37-50 I read about the life of Joseph, who by all accounts should have had an unforgiving heart. He endured hurt, pain, and betrayal at the hands of the people in his life. He was sold into slavery by his own brothers, was accused of rape, was forgotten in prison, yet gained favor with the Lord and was released to become a ruler of Egypt and prepared a nation to survive a famine. It was during that famine that he would encounter his brothers for the first time since they sold him into slavery.

Can you imagine being hated so much by your siblings or someone in your family that they would try to kill you? Would you be able to forgive that? But here Joseph finds himself face to face with his brothers, and now the tables are turned and their lives are in Joseph's hands. He had the power to turn them away and let them starve, but instead, he embraced them and chose to forgive. He says this in Genesis 50:19-21:

19 But Joseph replied, "Don't be afraid of me. Am I God, that I can punish you? **20 You intended to harm me, but God intended it all for good. He brought me to this position so I could save the** *lives of many people.* *²¹ No, don't be afraid. I will continue to take care of you and your children." So he reassured them by speaking kindly to them. - Genesis 50:19-21 (NLT) Emphasis Added*

FOR HIS GLORY

He says in Verse 20, You intended to harm me, but God intended it all for good. He brought me to this position so I could save the lives of many people. That's almost unbelievable, yet this is the precise scripture that brought it all together for me. What happened to me by the hand of the people in my life, whether it was family or friends had nothing to do with them, it was God who allowed the position I was in because it would allow me to write this book.

Without the hurt, pain, betrayal, loss and grief, I would never have been able to genuinely feel the hurt, the pain, the betrayal, the loss and the grief from the many women I encounter every day. I can genuinely grieve alongside them because I have been there.

Imagine if Joseph had decided not to forgive. Imagine if he had an unforgiving heart towards everyone in his life who had done him wrong? Would God have been able to use him for His glory? Would his brothers and their families have been saved from starvation? No, not at all. The story of Joseph helped me to understand that I didn't need to know why I had to go through what I went through. It no longer was my focus. My focus had changed to reflect how God could use me and my pain to help others.

I was finally able to think about every person who had caused me pain and forgive them knowing that God would get the glory. I was finally free. Have I forgiven everyone who has ever hurt me? Yes! Does it still hurt at times? Yes! The feelings will come, but I have decided when they do, I can speak life and pray and ask God to continue to help me with the process.

MAKE A DECISION:

Today, I forgive the people in my life who hurt me. I know that it may not make sense and that it is not for them, but it is for me, and

I deserve to be free. Today, I choose to walk in freedom, free from the hurt others have placed on me. I forgive myself for holding on to un-forgiveness and I ask you, Lord, to forgive me for being disobedient when your Word tells me to forgive those that trespassed against me. I am ready to do the work required to forgive, even when I don't feel like it.

_____

Signature

_____

Today's Date

NINE

I Had To Find Me

"Life isn't about finding yourself, it's about discovering who God created you to be."-author unknown

[5]*"Before I shaped you in the womb, I knew all about you. Before you saw the light of day, I had holy plans for you: A prophet to the nations—that's what I had in mind for you." - Jeremiah 1:5 (MSG)*

Me, a teacher? A preacher of the Gospel? A wife and First Lady? Never. Had you asked me twenty years ago if I would be a Pastor's wife, my answer would have been unequivocally NO! His mistress maybe, but certainly not a wife. I would never be proud of my thought process then, but it speaks to the hurting young woman I once was, who thought so little of herself that I would think I was only good enough to be a mistress and not a wife. However, despite my thought pattern then, I always knew that there was something inside of me that needed to come out. I never talked about it, but I would daydream about it all the time.

The Bible tells me in Psalms 139:14, that I am fearfully and wonderfully made and in Jeremiah 1:5, He knew me and had plans for me before I was even born. For me? Yes, for me. Let that sink in…He, had a plan for you before you even came into this world. He knew exactly who and what you were going to be. God is never surprised by your choices. Every choice you've made has been used by God to prepare you for your purpose. Even the choices that you thought were wrong were a necessary part of your training.

We are all created for a purpose, meaning we all have something that God wants us to do. Whatever it is can be as unique and different as we are. I believe that I was created to be a wife and a mother, but that is not where it ends. I believe I was also created to minister to broken and hurting women. You may have been created to encourage, to show compassion, or minster to the youth, the people on your job, your family, the elderly, or the homeless.

MIRROR MIRROR

What do you see when you look in the mirror? Do you see her? Do you like her? Do you love her? Do you see what God sees? For so many years I looked in the mirror and I couldn't answer yes to any of those questions. I didn't see me because I didn't know who I was. I didn't like who I was, I couldn't love myself, and I certainly couldn't see myself the way God saw me because I lived in constant condemnation. I convinced myself that God saw me as a sinner and a disappointment. I couldn't possibly be called a daughter of the King. I did not have an identity! My identity was based on the people around me. I defined myself by what I was called: wife, mother, daughter, sister, First Lady. My identity was rooted in what I was to others, not in Jesus Christ.

"The Person in the mirror is looking for the REAL YOU!" - Lady Victory Vernon

But here is the good news, God sees beyond who we are right now, instead He sees who we will become. He loves both who we are today, and who we are becoming. He just loves us. Christ died for us while we were sinners. He didn't wait and say, no, I'm not ready to die yet because I need you to get it together first.

⁸But God showed his great love for us by sending Christ to die for us while we were still sinners. -Romans 5:8 (NLT)

God loves you-in spite of the fact that you are not where you think you should be.
God loves you-in spite of your sins.
God loves you-in spite of your flaws.
God loves you so much that He sacrificed His son for YOU.

The scripture goes on to tell us that because we live under grace, the free gift that He has given us, we no longer live under condemnation. He gave us a free gift---one that is never earned, we can't work for it, He gives it to us even when we think we do not deserve it.

¹⁶And the result of God's gracious gift is very different from the result of that one man's sin. For Adam's sin led to condemnation, but God's free gift leads to our being made right with God, even though we are guilty of many sins. -Romans 5:16 (NLT)

IN HIS IMAGE

If you want to see yourself the way God sees you, if you want to make sure that you are indeed created in His image, I pray you follow these steps.

Step 1 - Accept Jesus as your Lord and Savior. If you have not yet accepted Jesus Christ as your Lord and Savior, and never said the Prayer of Salvation, I invite you today to pray this prayer:

"Father, I am a sinner. I am truly sorry, and now I want to turn away from my sinful life toward you. Please forgive me. I believe that your son, Jesus Christ,

died for my sins, was resurrected from the dead, is alive, and hears my prayer. I invite Jesus to become the Lord of my life, to rule and reign in my heart from this day forward. Please send your Holy Spirit to help me obey You, and to do Your will for the rest of my life. In Jesus' name I pray, Amen."

If this is the first time you have said this prayer, I welcome you to the family of God, and if this is a re-dedication, welcome back! I encourage you now to find a local church where you can be baptized and grow in the knowledge of God through His Word, the Bible.

Step 2 - Believe by faith you are who God says you are-- His child. Know what the scriptures say about you. Repeat after me:

- I am a child of God - [12]But to all who believed him and accepted him, he gave the right to become children of God, -John 1:12 (NLT)
- I am chosen and dearly loved - [16] You didn't choose me. I chose you. I appointed you to go and produce lasting fruit, so that the Father will give you whatever you ask for, using my name. -John 15:16 (NLT)
- I am a new creation- [17]This means that anyone who belongs to Christ has become a new person. The old life is gone; a new life has begun. -2 Cor 5:17 (NLT)
- I am the righteousness of Christ -[21]God made him who had no sin to be sin for us, so that in him we might become the righteousness of God. -2 Cor 5:21 (NIV)
- I am healed by His stripes - [24]He himself bore our sins in his body on the cross, so that we might die to sins and live for righteousness; by his wounds you have been healed. -1 Peter 2:24 (NIV)
- I am a joint heir with Jesus -[14]For all who are led by the Spirit of God are children of God. -Romans 8:14 (NLT)
- I am more than a conqueror - [37]No, in all these things we are more than conquerors through him who loved us. - Rom 8:37 (NIV)

- I am righteous and holy - [24]Put on your new nature, created to be like God—truly righteous and holy. Eph 4:24 (NLT)
- I am dearly loved - [12]Since God chose you to be the holy people he loves, you must clothe yourselves with tenderhearted mercy, kindness, humility, gentleness, and patience. -Col 3:12 (NLT)
- I am completely forgiven - [9]But if we confess our sins to him, he is faithful and just to forgive us our sins and to cleanse us from all wickedness. -1 John 1:9 (NLT)
- I am totally free - [36]So if the Son sets you free, you are truly free. -John 8:36 (NLT)
- I am uniquely designed - [14]Thank you for making me so wonderfully complex! Your workmanship is marvelous— how well I know it. -Psalm 139:14 (NLT)
- It is not I who live, but Christ lives in me - [20]My old self has been crucified with Christ. It is no longer I who live, but Christ lives in me. So I live in this earthly body by trusting in the Son of God, who loved me and gave himself for me. -Gal 2:20 (NLT)
- I am an overcomer - [11]"...And they have defeated him by the blood of the Lamb and by their testimony"-Rev 12:11 (NLT)

These are only a few of the promises of God and you may not believe these truths overnight, but you will eventually, if you keep meditating and speaking the promises over your life. Whenever the enemy tells you who you are not, remind him who God says you are. I promise the more you speak God's Word over your own life, the more you will believe and trust Him. You must put His Word into practice in your daily life.

[24]*Therefore everyone who hears these words of mine and puts them into practice is like a wise man who built his house on the rock.* [25]*The rain came down, the streams rose, and the winds blew and beat against that house; yet it did not fall, because it had its foundation on the rock." -Matthew 7:24-25 (NIV)*

He tells us clearly that if we put His Word into practice we are wise and no matter what the enemy may throw at us...especially our past and our feelings.... we will not fall because we have built a solid foundation in Christ.

Step 3 - Surrender to His will-- This has been the hardest for me to do. Surrendering can be very tough, especially if you have been the victim of abuse of any kind. This is surrendering to our Heavenly Father who loves us, who will never leave us, who only wants the best for us. For many years, I didn't understand what surrender really meant. In case you are like me, here it is:

Surrendering your life to Him means:

- Trusting God's purpose without understanding the circumstances of how, why, when, and what.
- Following God's lead without knowing where He is sending you.
- Waiting on God's timing without any idea of when it will happen.
- Expecting your prayers to be answered without knowing how God will provide.

We say it all the time, 'let go and let God", what that means is relying on Him to work things out for you, instead of you trying to manipulate or control people or the situation around you or forcing your agenda. It is when you can take a step back and instead of trying harder, you trust Him to take care of you.

How can you practice surrendering today? Easy, practice it in your daily relationships. Instead of defending yourself when faced with adversity, don't react to the criticism, stop defending yourself and allow God to defend you. Don't be self-serving. Instead, ask "How can I serve others?" Don't shine the light on yourself, instead allow God to shine His light on you.

When you finally recognize who you are in Christ, His beloved daughter, not perfect but perfectly working on being better day-by-day, you will be able to look in the mirror, even on days when all is not right and boldly proclaim, "I AM HIS, AND HE LOVES ME," and that is enough for me.

THE PURPOSE

God has created us all with a purpose, you, me, your parents, your children...everyone. It is up to us to seek His help to discover what that purpose is and then we must decide to walk in it. Over the last sixteen years in ministry, I have found that many of us are very confused about what our purpose is. Is it a calling? Is it my talent? Is it my gift? Is it what comes easy or natural to me? I believe that our purpose is "that thing that makes you come alive". It is the place where our greatest passion, our talents and gifts intersect. It is that place where we are freely being us. It's the place where we feel alive, the place where we feel God in and through us.

⁶We have different gifts, according to the grace given to each of us. If your gift is prophesying, then prophesy in accordance with your faith; ⁷if it is serving, then serve; if it is teaching, then teach; ⁸ if it is to encourage, then give encouragement; if it is giving, then give generously; if it is to lead, do it diligently; if it is to show mercy, do it cheerfully." -Romans 12:6-8 (NIV)

This scripture tells us that we all have a spiritual gift, mine may be different from yours and yours may be different from your friends, but the truth remains, we all have a gift, and it is up to us to ask the Holy Spirit to reveal them to us. It is important to understand that spiritual gifts are not innate, natural talents that we are born with, but rather are empowerments by the Holy Spirt to minster in a way that would not be possible by our natural efforts. These spiritual gifts are given to us to help build, edify and empower the building of the Church and extending the Kingdom of God.

Ruth Soukup a contributor to the Proverbs31.org devotionals says it this way: "Finding your gift often means a messy process of finding, then learning how to embrace the God-given talents you already have, rather than those you wish you had. It means discovering what you enjoy and are truly good at, then determining how to merge talent and abilities with the ideas, dreams and pursuits you are most passionate about. And sometimes finding your sweet spot means taking a wrong turn — or even failing along the way."[10]

"Failing along the way", now I could connect with that, because I felt that is what I was doing for the first ten years in ministry, failing while trying to identify my spiritual gifts. I knew what I was good at; I was administrative, faithful, a hard worker, and a great team player. I immersed myself in ministry opportunities that allowed me to hide. I preferred to be behind the scenes, mainly because I was always afraid that I didn't know enough; I simply felt unqualified. Even though I served faithfully in children's church, finance, set-up and break down, hospitality, you name it, I didn't feel fulfilled. I always had this nagging feeling that I wasn't in the right place.

God however, spoke loud and clear to me through other people, situations, and my vision and dreams. My Pastor and others in leadership would ask me to lead a bible study, introduce a speaker, call members that needed encouragement, and I would decline letting it be known that I wasn't ready. After declining I always felt like a failure or that I had let them down. Deep down I knew this was exactly what God was calling me to do. He had given me the gift of teaching, serving, and encouragement and I was running from it. I recognize now that I wasn't really running, but that it was God's way of preparing me for my purpose. It was part of my training.

DREAMS & VISIONS

For as long as I can remember, I have had very vivid colorful dreams. I have reoccurring dreams, I can dream, wake up, go back to sleep and continue the same dream. On occasion, I will have the same dreams I had in my early childhood. For most of my life I felt as if my dreams were a burden. I started to research dreams and their meanings to get an understanding of what they meant. The more I researched, the more frustrated I became because the "dream interpretation" would be the opposite of what I felt, and this caused me to be confused. Along with my dreams, I also had visions of conversations or places that resembled déjà vu moments. As a child, I kept these to myself because I had the feeling people would think I was odd, different or even crazy, so I processed them on my own or simply dismissed them.

Somewhere around my early teens, my dreams and visions would become more prominent and I began to pay attention to the details. I started journaling and it helped me cope with the craziness around me. One dream stood out. I was standing on my junior high school's auditorium stage speaking to students about my life, achievements, setbacks, and how I endured despite my circumstances. I would see myself standing behind a podium in a black suit, black high heels with my hair combed back in a bun. After the presentation, young girls would come up to me and tell me how I inspired them to never give up and then they would share their stories and struggles. At that point in my life I had struggled, but nothing like what was to come. I used to think, what does this mean? Was I going to be a teacher? A principal perhaps?

It was this particular dream that finally came to fruition twenty years later when my husband being led by the Holy Spirit, decided to move the Church from our gym into a high school auditorium. After his first visit, he was so excited, he described every detail from the lights, to the stage, to the chairs and the color of the curtain. That night I went to bed and couldn't sleep, my dream from middle school kept coming back to me, every detail my husband described was in my dream. I couldn't comprehend it. I prayed to God that night and asked Him to finally reveal what this dream was all about.

The next morning, we drove to the high school, and as we walked from the parking lot to the entrance of the building I noticed the railing, which looked familiar. As I touched it I saw myself standing on the stage, holding onto a brown podium looking in the audience with the lights shining in my eyes. I felt like I couldn't breathe.

I didn't know what to do, and at that moment my husband looked over to me and asked, "Are you okay?" I pulled myself together and proceeded to walk inside the auditorium. I was speechless, what God revealed twenty years' prior had come to pass. As I walked down the aisle, there was a brown podium sitting off to the side and red curtains flanking each side of the stage. Once on stage, I stood behind the podium, at the exact time a janitor turned on the lights. I had to blink several times to allow my eyes to adjust. It was right then and there that God spoke to my spirit and said, "I showed you this so many years ago because I needed you to get ready. I needed you to see yourself over the years, so when I made it happen you would not be afraid. Trust me and I will show you."

I don't know how God will reveal your purpose, but I do know that He will. It's scary, I know; however, when you follow His guidance and His ways, you will be able to accomplish anything. One of my favorite sayings is this: "If God gave you the vision, He will give you the provision." I no longer worry about the how. How will it get done? How is this going to work out? I only focus on what He told me to do, I trust God to make the rest happen. He will show me who to talk to and who to go to for help. I am no longer worried or freaked out.

FREE INDEED

^{36} *So if the Son sets you free, you will be free indeed. -John 8:36 (NIV)*

When someone asks my husband how are you? Or how's it going? He always responds with, "I'm living LIFE! I'm Living in Freedom Every Day." This is a quote that he borrowed from his good friend, motivational speaker and author, Ken Brown. My husband chooses to live in freedom every day even when things are challenging. He does this because he understands what living in freedom means. It's not about how he feels, but about that truth that God set him free.

The world defines freedom as a life without restraint; the same way I did when I finally moved out of my parents' house into my own place. I finally had the freedom to do anything I wanted to do and say anything I wanted to say, and there was nobody who could tell me otherwise. I was grown and I could do what I wanted. Back then I may have felt like I was living in freedom doing what I wanted when I wanted, yet the truth was, I was still secretly living in fear, guilt, worry, bitterness and bondage.

Truly living in freedom is freedom from fear, free from guilt, free from worry, free from bitterness and free from bondage. True freedom is no longer pretending and being free in who you are. This type of freedom is only possible by getting to know Christ intimately, by walking in His ways and accepting the changes He is making in and through us. I had to realize that my life was no longer my own. It wasn't about what I needed or wanted, it was and is all about what He wants and needs from me. His will, not mine.

MAKE A DECISION:

Today, I will look in the mirror and commit to loving myself the way my Heavenly Father does. I will speak His Word and His promises over my life. I will remind myself daily who I am in Him. I will remember that I am created in His image and when I mess up (because I know I will) I will go to Him and repent. I will walk in the purpose that He has given me and if I am not sure yet what that is, I will diligently search to find it by asking Him. I will commit to praying and reading His Word so it can be hidden in my heart. I will believe by faith that I am truly FREE INDEED.

_____

Signature

_____

Today's Date

TEN

I Had To Die To Self

"Death is a necessary prelude to resurrection. To bear long-term fruit for Christ, we need to recognize that some things must die so something new can grow."
— *Peter Scazzero*

TRUST HIM

"It's time to trust Him, you've done your work and you are still here, but now the real work starts." These were the words from my counselor after I had completed my grief recovery work. I had hoped I was done with the work, but I knew better. I still had to learn how to navigate my life moving forward, knowing that this would be a new normal for me. I knew that my "change" would have meant nothing if I didn't do the work required for me to become healthy while trusting God in the process.

3 Trust in the Lord with all your heart, and do not lean on your own understanding; 6 in all your ways acknowledge him, and he will make your path straight. - Proverbs 3:5-6 (NIV)

I was finally ready to walk the "straight path". I was tired of detours and knew I would have to trust Him completely. Even though I felt such inner peace as it related to my past, I knew that there was more work that needed to be done. I hadn't finished, this was just the start. As I was sitting in my prayer room one morning, the Lord clearly spoke into my spirit that I needed to change.

"What?" I was perplexed. I responded with, "That's what I've been doing the last two years. What do you mean? I'm done. I did my work; the counselor said so. Yes, I was arguing with God once again. I became quiet and asked God to show me what He meant.

He had me pull out a notebook and write these words, "I HAD TO CHANGE". He continued to tell me that I had done the easy work, but that now the hard work was coming. He said I needed to share my process with others. He said this wasn't only about me, but every woman that needed to change. He told me that my work will never be in vain. He said, "trust Me", but there is one more thing you need to do. I knew exactly what He was going to say: SURRENDER.

SURRENDER

What do you think when you hear the word surrender? Does it conjure up images of you coming out with your hands up? Is it waving the white flag? Is it allowing someone else to dictate what you can and can't do? Is it someone else having total control over you? These were my thoughts from my past, because it only related to surrendering to people or the wrong things. At this point in my walk with God I knew that He only wanted the best for me, and it wasn't about me losing control, but about me allowing Him to take the lead.

The biggest battle we face with surrender is not the battle on the outside but the real war that goes on inside of us when it comes to giving up our will and giving it to God. As Christians we say it all the time, "Your will God, not mine," but do we really know what that means? I don't think so, because if we did, none of us would ever have a problem surrendering.

What is surrender? I asked God, what are you really asking me to do? He led me to Luke Chapter One, when an angel appeared to Mary who would become the mother of Jesus and announced God's plan for her life.

Imagine this…God sends you an angel, says you are pregnant and the baby will become the savior of the world. How would you react? I'm not certain, but I'm guessing your response would be something like, "Me? But I'm a virgin, how can this happen? Me? The mother of Jesus, I don't think so. I'm not worthy, I'm not holy enough. You don't know my past, what I've been through, what I've done".

Sound familiar? Isn't this how we respond when God asks us to step out of our comfort zone? But here is what I love about this story, here is Mary's response:

> [38] "I am the Lord's servant," Mary answered. "May your word to me be fulfilled." Then the angel left her. –Luke 1:38 (NIV)

Her first and only response to the angel was one of surrender. She said, "I am the Lord's servant." That is incredible. Imagine doing this without saying or thinking, "Let me pray about this," as we do so often.

Mary shows us what a life of complete and utter surrender looks like. She surrendered to God's will even though it didn't make sense. How could she have a child without being married and being a virgin? She surrendered to God's will even though it was difficult. She didn't think about what people would say, she simply responded with, "May your word to me be fulfilled." Mary surrendered.

What was God asking me to surrender? I knew exactly what He was asking. He wanted me to be transparent…transparent with my past, continuous struggle in dealing with my feelings and emotions. I was growing spiritually, but emotionally I still had a lot of work to do.

> "Emotional health and spiritual maturity are inseparable. It is not possible to be spiritually mature while remaining emotionally immature." — Peter Scazzero[11]

While reading the book "Emotionally Healthy Spirituality" by Peter Scazzero, I finally understood what God was saying to me. I had spent so much time, working on becoming a better Christian by following the rules and then working through my grief issues, that I neglected my inner-self and my emotions. There were days when I was blindsided by emotions that would show up unexpectantly.

For instance, whenever someone left our Church, I became very emotional, even depressed as I wondered if it had something to do with me. These were the emotions and feelings connected to my abandonment issues that showed up whenever someone exited my life. I would then internalize it and all the people who previously left my life came flooding back to my mind. I would become emotional, not knowing how to deal with these feelings of sadness and anger. I would spiritualize them away with thoughts like "Well, obviously, God didn't want them in our lives." This could very well have been the truth, but I didn't know how to reign in my feelings and ended up being an emotional wreck. I realized I was missing a very important gift God has given us all - The fruit of the Spirit.

[22] But the Holy Spirit produces this kind of fruit in our lives: love, joy, peace, patience, kindness, goodness, faithfulness, [23] gentleness, and self-control. There is no law against these things! -Galatians 5:22-23 (NLT)

I had to learn to walk daily in love, joy, peace, patience, kindness, goodness, faithfulness, gentleness and self-control, no matter what was going on around me. I had to surrender to His will, His way of doing things no matter how I felt or what I thought.

What is God asking you to surrender to? Your flesh, your emotions, your mouth, your heart? I ask that you earnestly seek Him in prayer and ask Him to show you, before it comes out sideways, and believe me, it will.

DIE TO SELF

[25] For whoever wishes to save his life will lose it; but whoever loses his life for My sake will find it. —Matthew 16:25 (NASB)

To die to self is to set aside what we want in that moment and focus instead on loving God and valuing others as highly as we value ourselves. God was asking me to move from self-centeredness *(my issues, my problems, what I went through, who hurt me)* to becoming an open-hearted follower of Christ who cares deeply for others *(their issues, their problems, what they went through and who hurt them)*. When we practice this daily it becomes easier and we can see beyond our own needs and give our focus and attention to the needs of others. My husband always tells our congregation, that we as a people are so self-focused that we are unable to be Kingdom focused.

But how do I do this? How do I die to self daily without neglecting the care of my spiritual and emotional health? Jesus describes to us how to do this when He says:

²⁴If anyone wishes to come after Me, he must deny himself, and take up his cross and follow Me." -Matthew 16:24 (NASB)

Yes, we must take up our own cross and follow Him. What was my cross? All my mess, my junk, my struggles, my issues, I had to take them and still follow Him. In spite of all I've been through, He still wanted me to follow Him. He goes on further to say:

²For whoever wishes to save his life will lose it; but whoever loses his life for My sake will find it." -Matthew 16:25 (NASB)

There it was, the hope I was looking for. By surrendering and following Him I will find my life--the abundant life He promised me! And the same promise applies to you.

Please do not confuse dying to self to self-denial or self-rejection. God treasures your divinely created self. He doesn't want to kill the part of you that makes you uniquely you. God works within you, reshapes you into the renewed person you were meant to be. Learning to die to self daily made my life easier because I've learned to be content even when I feel like I'm not being heard, overlooked or rejected. Dying to self, allowed me to focus on God and how He would want me to respond. I ask myself often, can I be secure in God's love without recognition? Is God's approval enough for me, or do I still look for and fish for compliments when I believe I did something great or admirable? Can I allow God to oversee my reputation, or do I still feel the need to defend myself when someone is talking about me or questioning my motives?

PEACE

[33]I have told you all this so that you may have peace in me. Here on earth you will have many trials and sorrows. But take heart, because I have overcome the world. -John 16:33 (NLT)

Jesus is teaching his disciples that peace is found in Him and Him alone. The security of the disciples rested on their ability to understand what Jesus was saying to them. Jesus had been preparing them for what was to come. He was telling them that the time was almost there, when He would go to be with the Father and that they would scatter. The disciples felt a sense of security because they answered Jesus by saying:

[29]At last you are speaking plainly and not figuratively [30]Now we understand that you know everything, and there's no need to question you. From this we believe that you came from God." -John 16:29-30 (NLT)

Up to this point, my peace was always conditional. I always wanted to know, why? Why am I going through this? Why is this happening? When I didn't get an answer, I would feel no peace. God started to reveal to me through this scripture that I could have peace even without understanding why. I didn't need to question Him, but have complete trust in Him. The peace I was seeking was in Him.

This encouraged me to stop trying to get the answers to feel peace, but instead focus on peace despite the circumstances and troubles surrounding me. And I want to encourage you today. Peace is found in Jesus, not our understanding of the cause of our troubles, but in Him alone. If you have made the choice to change, you must know where your peace comes from because without it, you will never reach contentment in the change you made.

CHANGED

This journey of change was not easy and it will not be easy for you. It will take time, full surrender, obedience, and submission to God's will for your life. It will require calling out to Him for help, strength and guidance. It will shake up your foundation, change your mind and your heart. It will make people walk away from you and you walk away from them. It will take you out of your comfort zone, but it will be well worth the journey.

God has brought a great reward in my life in recompense for the hurt, pain, abuse and loss I suffered in my early life. I now can live the abundant life of freedom. God is blessing me; He is opening doors for me; He's giving me opportunities I never thought I could have or even deserve. He makes me happy and brings me joy even during trouble.

Trusting God will bring justice into your life for the Lord God gives us a promise that says:

[7]Instead of shame and dishonor, you will enjoy a double share of honor. You will possess a double portion of prosperity in your land, and everlasting joy will be yours. -Isaiah 61:7 (NLT)

Because of what I've been through, because of what you have been through, God will give you a double portion of prosperity if you trust Him. If you are living a life now where you are stuck because someone mistreated you, hurt you, rejected you, abandoned you, or abused you — Remind yourself of this promise — A double portion blessing is on the way. Your latter will be greater if CHANGE is what you seek and if change is what you choose.

"When remembering where you were, when understanding where you are, when

knowing where you want to be, you should be able to boldly look in the mirror and repeat: I Had to Change! – Quotucated

MAKE A DECISION:

Today, I decide that I HAVE TO CHANGE. I will die to my flesh daily, I will pick up my cross and follow Christ, whether I feel like it or not. I will trust Him and not in my feelings. I will remind myself that I may not be where I want to be, yet I will rejoice in the fact that I am not where I used to be. I will celebrate small accomplishments and intentionally look for peace in Him. I surrender my will for His and as I am changing, I am reminding myself of the double portion promise that is to come.

_____

Signature

_____

Today's Date

References

1. James, John W. and Friedman, Russell. The Grief
   Recovery Handbook. New York, NY, HarperCollins
   Books, 2009.
2. Kendall, Jackie. Surrender Your Junior God Badge:
   Every Woman's Battle with Control. Shippenburg, PA,
   Destiny Imaging Publishing, 2015.
3. www.Miriam-webster.com, accessed February 2017,
   https://www.merriam-webster.com/dictionary/patterns
4. Yerkes, Mary J. "Destructive Conflict: Recognize It. Stop
   it. Focusonthefamily.com, accessed May 2017,
   https://www.focusonthefamily.com/lifechallenges/relationship-
   challenges/conflict-resolution/destructive-conflict-
   recognize-it-stop-it.htmp
5. Knowles, Solange. "Cranes in the Sky". A Seat at the
   Table. MP3. Saint Records and Columbia Records,
   http://www.songlyrics.com/solange/cranes-in-the-sky-
   lyrics/
6. James, John W. and Friedman, Russell. The Grief
   Recovery Handbook. New York, NY, HarperCollins
   Books, 2009.

7. James, John W. and Friedman, Russell. The Grief Recovery Handbook. New York, NY, HarperCollins Books, 2009.

8. James, John W. and Friedman, Russell. The Grief Recovery Handbook. New York, NY, HarperCollins Books, 2009.

9. James, Cole "The Key Benefits of Forgiving During the Grieving Process. Thegriefrecoverymethod.com, accessed June 2017, http://blog.griefrecoverymethod.com/forgiveness-during-the-grieving-process

10. Soukup, Ruth. "Finding your Sweetspot. Proverbs31.org, accessed April 2017, http://proverbs31.org/devotions/devo/finding-your-sweet-spot-2/

11. Scazzero, Peter. Emotionally Healthy Spirituality. Grand Rapids, MI, Zondervan, 2014.

About the Author

Charlet Lewis, affectionately referred to as "Lady Charlet," is the wife of Tony Lewis, Senior Pastor of Light of Life Church, a ministry focused on the least, the lost and the left out. Lady Charlet serves alongside her husband to ensure that his God-given assignments are carried out. She is a licensed and ordained minister of the gospel and a Certified Grief Recovery Specialist®. Her own journey through grief recovery after the loss of her mother has allowed her the compassion to guide anyone struggling with loss towards their own healing and recovery.

She is known for her transparency, endless love, wisdom and humor, which she pours unreservedly into any one she meets. Her passion is to help women discover their God-given potential and purpose. Using her no-nonsense candor, Lady Charlet often uses creative illustrations and concepts from her own life to inspire, encourage, advocate and teach. Her teachings inspire and challenge women to develop a strong relationship with God and to strive toward emotional and spiritual health.

She is the Director of Light of Life Church Women's Ministry, hosts a yearly Women's Conference called "#IHAD2CHANGE", and co-hosts a weekly Radio Show with her husband called "The

Pastor Tony Lewis Show – Your Health is your Wealth" on Kingdom Sound Radio. She is an avid reader, writer and blogger.

She is a woman of true character, and she handles her obligation to serve in ministry alongside her husband of 17 years with superb devotion. She is the proud mom of 2 boys and 2 girls ages 23, 16, 11 and 7. She homeschools 2 of the 4 and takes her daily responsibilities serious yet with a healthy dose of humor and fun.

To Connect with or invite
Lady Charlet to speak at your next event:

www.ladycharlet.com

https://www.facebook.com/IHadToChange
https://www.twitter.com/ladycharlet
https://www.instagram.com/ladycharlet/

Made in the USA
Middletown, DE
26 November 2017